Preaching Conversations with Scholars

Preaching Conversations with Scholars
The Preacher as Scholar

Edited by
Rodney Wallace Kennedy

WIPF & STOCK · Eugene, Oregon

PREACHING CONVERSATIONS WITH SCHOLARS
The Preacher as Scholar

Copyright © 2016 Rodney Wallace Kennedy. All rights reserved. Except for brief quotations in critical publications or reviews, no part of this book may be reproduced in any manner without prior written permission from the publisher. Write: Permissions, Wipf and Stock Publishers, 199 W. 8th Ave., Suite 3, Eugene, OR 97401.

Wipf & Stock
An Imprint of Wipf and Stock Publishers
199 W. 8th Ave., Suite 3
Eugene, OR 97401

www.wipfandstock.com

PAPERBACK ISBN: 978-1-4982-9073-9
HARDCOVER ISBN: 978-1-4982-9075-3
EBOOK ISBN: 978-1-4982-9074-6

Manufactured in the U.S.A.   OCTOBER 6, 2016

Contents

Contributors | vii

Preface | ix

Introduction | xiii

1 The Gospel Is Relevant | 1
   Response by Steve Harmon | 6

2 God Is Good! | 11
   Response by Herbie Miller | 16

3 Excel in Generosity | 20
   Response by Elizabeth Newman | 25
   Response by Emily Hunter McGowin | 25

4 A Scary Resurrection | 31
   Response by William Portier | 36

5 Guess Who's Coming to Dinner | 39
   Response by David-Wheeler Reed | 45

6 What Have We Done with the Good News? | 49
   Response by Philip E. Thompson | 55

7 Is There an Unforgivable Sin? | 58
   Response by Derek Hatch | 63

8 Sabbath Gospel | 67

      Response by Mark Ryan | 71

9 Welcome to the Family | 77

      Response by Brad Kallenberg | 82

10 Are American Christians Persecuted? | 87

      Response by William Vance Trollinger, Jr. | 93

      Response by Susan L. Trollinger | 96

11 Jesus and ISUS | 100

      Response by Kyle Childress | 108

12 The Holy Spirit as Reading Teacher | 111

      Response by Jason Hentschel | 116

13 Theology as Twitter | 119

      Response by Ethan Smith | 124

Bibliography | 129

Contributors

Kyle Childress is Pastor of Austin Heights Baptist Church in Nacogdoches, Texas.

Steven Harmon is Visiting Associate Professor of Historical Theology at Gardner Webb University School of Divinity in Boiling Springs, North Carolina.

Derek Hatch is Professor Cristian Studies at Howard Payne University in Brownwood, Texas.

Jason Hentschel is a Lecturer in Religious Studies at the University of Dayton in Dayton, Ohio.

Brad Kallenberg is Professor of Ethics at the University of Dayton in Dayton, Ohio.

Herbie Miller is the Interim Pastor of Corinth Presbyterian Church and recently earned his PhD from the Department of Religious Studies at the University of Dayton in Dayton, Ohio.

Emily McGowin is a PhD graduate in Religious Studies at the University of Dayton in Dayton, Ohio.

Elizabeth Newman is Professor of Theology and Ethics at Baptist Theological Seminary of Richmond in Richmond, Virginia.

William Portier is Professor of Theology at the University of Dayton in Dayton, Ohio.

David Wheeler Reed is a Research Fellow at Yale Divinity School in New Haven, Connecticut.

Mark Ryan is lecturer in Ethics at the University of Dayton in Dayton, Ohio.

CONTRIBUTORS

Ethan Smith is a PhD student in religious studies at the University of Dayton in Dayton, Ohio.

Philip Thompson is Professor of Theology at Sioux Falls Seminary in Sioux Falls, South Dakota.

Susan Trollinger is Professor of English at the University of Dayton in Dayton, Ohio.

William Vance Trollinger, Jr. is Professor of History at the University of Dayton in Dayton, Ohio.

Preface

This book is the story of a small group, a church, a university, and a baptist preacher. The book came to life over a period of nine years over coffee and conversations with friends, colleagues, and scholars. The book contains sermons that bear my name as author but the sermons are really sustained conversations that reflect the insights of my fellow contributors, especially those who willingly listened to me preach Sunday after Sunday at the First Baptist Church of Dayton, Ohio. This then is the story of Rodney Wallace Kennedy relating to the First Baptist Church of Dayton and the University of Dayton—a perfect match for this catholic/baptist.

In one sense this is a provincial book since it revolves around two local communities: the First Baptist Church of Dayton and the University of Dayton. Here a Baptist Church and a Catholic University engaged in multiple partnerships that I believe mutually enriched both institutions. The majority of the contributors to this book are members of First Baptist Dayton or professors or graduate students at the University of Dayton. In some cases they are part of both communities. The other contributors have written essays for other books that I have edited. My hope for this book is its provincial origin will turn out to have universal application.

This is also a deeply personal book because it is the product of a story, and believing as I do that we don't exist without stories, I need to tell you at least part of this one story. The story behind the book deserves telling not only to ground the reader in the how and why and thus imparting a better understanding but because the backstory is itself the incarnation of the words that fill this book. Start with a small group that meets every Monday evening at 7:00 p.m. in the home of Bill and Sue Trollinger. Bill is a history professor and Sue is an English professor at the University of Dayton. Add to that group Brad Kallenberg, ethics professor at the University of Dayton.

PREFACE

The group also includes Ed and Sharon Wingham, Jeanne Kallenberg, and my wife, Johnelle Kennedy. The format of the group was to begin with Evening Prayer and then read the lectionary lessons for the next Sunday. After a time of discussion, questions, and some bits of disagreements, we spent time in prayer. If ever there was a group of people who deserve to be called "my saving group," it is this group. Carlyle Marney taught me to choose my priest from among thousands, and in my case, I was greedy and chose these seven persons to be my priests. Some of us simply require more priests. Each Monday I was given the freedom to "come undone," be myself, and soak in the insights of my priests. Without them I don't think I would have survived the "sweet agony" of the preaching ministry.

An additional part of the story borders on what might be considered a miracle. After all, how likely is it that a group of Ph.D. students from a Catholic university would become members of the First Baptist Church of Dayton? Knowing of no other usable category, I credit the providence of God with bringing a brilliant group of young baptist scholars to the Ph.D. program at the University of Dayton. These young scholars became members of First Baptist Church and gave to my life what St. Paul calls the "amazing riches of the grace of God." I am indebted to Derek Hatch, Andy Black, Jason Hentschel, Lucas Martin, Ethan Smith, Jordan Fannin, and Coleman Fannin for their amazing contributions to the First Baptist Church and to my life as a pastor/preacher/teacher.

This book attempts to combine the weekly discipline of preaching in one particular pulpit—The First Regular Baptist Church of Dayton, Ohio—with the insights and conversations of a number of scholarly partners. I would be remiss if I didn't at least to attempt to help the reader understand that the concept of a "free pulpit" finds it penultimate expression at the First Baptist Church of Dayton, Ohio. The congregation of First Baptist Church not only says they have a free pulpit, but they make it possible for the preacher to say whatever the Spirit has put on his/her heart. What a glorious congregation! What an amazing people of God!

Long an intellectual bastion among American Baptists thanks to the more than three decades of the faithful pastorate of Dr. Charles Seasholes First Baptist Church gave me the freedom to push the boundaries. As Bill Trollinger says in the history of First Baptist Dayton:

> With a doctorate from Newton (now Andover Newton) Seminary, Seasholes was a charter member of the Roger Williams Fellowship, a liberal group in the American Baptist Convention that prized

PREFACE

diversity of opinion on the denomination, and that was committed to the notion that "the New Testament is the all-sufficient ground of our faith and practice" (which of course D. S. Burnet and the Campbellites proclaimed at First Baptist in 1829, much to the consternation of the "faithful eight"!) Seasholes was also very involved in the ecumenical movement, even serving as a delegate to the initial meeting of the World Council of Churches in 1948. At First Baptist Seasholes introduced the practice of ministers and choir wearing robes and organized Wednesday evening lectures on world problems and Sunday evening book review discussions. He served on innumerable city committees and boards, helped bring Planned Parenthood to Dayton, and presided over Orville Wright's funeral in January of 1948.

I have attempted to maintain faithful continuity to Dr. Seasholes. When I came to First Baptist Dayton, I realized that Dr. Seasholes was the one pastor to reach the status of "beloved," the pastor with whom all of us who came after him were compared. Early in my ministry at First Baptist, I asked the congregation to adopt an annual Jazz Worship Sunday. In offering a reason for this recommendation I said, "As you know Dr. Seasholes still resides in the attic and from time-to-time I seek his advice. When I told him I wanted to have a Jazz Worship Sunday, he said, "You go, son!" I knew that I had arrived when one lady told me after church, "Dr. Seasholes would have never said such a thing." The good Dr. and I then gladly shared the pulpit and attic for the next thirteen years.

To be a preacher is to be joined, to be put in conversation with others—both here and now and with those who went before us. The telling and retelling of our stories enriches our lives. One of the remarkable discoveries of my journey in preaching is that my preaching improves as the engagement of the audience intensifies. An old-time evangelist once told my home town congregation, "If you want better preaching, you should pray better prayers." I would add that we should add more intense and more determined challenging conversations. In fact, let's push the envelope to say that the congregation needs to demand better preaching.

Through conversations with so many scholars I know that I have been made more of a preacher than I could ever try to be on my own. I owe a great debt of gratitude to my conversation partners, who with some gentle persuasion were willing to critique my sermons. I know this would not have been possible without my colleagues who read my sermons and wrote reflections. Even more I am indebted to those who, as faithful members

PREFACE

of First Baptist Church, not only read my sermons, but listened to them each week. I will never be able to repay with enough gratitude the encouragement of Bill and Sue Trollinger, Brad Kallenberg, Derek Hatch, Jason Hentschel, Mark Ryan, and Lucas Martin as well as their contributions to this book. In addition, I am grateful to Jacob H. Don, professor of history emeritus, Wright State University and Roy Vice, history professor at Wright State University for listening to my sermons and engaging me in conversations that connected theology and history.

My connection with scholars has at least caused some of the scholarship to rub off on me. After all, the church's first five centuries were made possible by Christian scholars and in spite of the difficult relationship that now exists between church and academy I am committed to the partnership of church and academy. Scholars are one of God's most important gifts to the church. God has given us historians to make sure we remember those who practiced holy and faithful living in the past. A church disconnected from scholarship may die or retire whichever one is the least painful. Of course, I am aware that this may be considered elitist, but that is not a concern that I can manufacture in my heart or my mind. I simply cannot fathom attempting to preach without attempting to be as scholarly as possible. Scholarship is a gift not a curse and it certainly doesn't deserve the bitter criticism that it receives in certain Christian communities in the USA.

This book represents my deepest and most sacred convictions about the glorious art of preaching and its necessary relationship to preachers who having read a book read another and another and another. Preaching and conversations about preaching keep the tradition alive and well. My hope is that the sermons exhibited here and the critiques offered will challenge all who preach to ever more intense and intellectual pursuit of sermonic efforts.

Introduction

FOR REASONS THAT BEDEVIL my imagination, segments of the American Christian scene have an allergic reaction to critical scholarship. Sermons at times are dedicated to the disemboweling of all scholarship, and a skepticism toward biblical scholarship, science, history, and economics has blossomed in the pews. This is not anti-intellectualism; it is anti-scholarship, in particular a strange mistrust of the scholarship of our universities and seminaries. Responding to this badly informed and harmful trend gave the original impetus for this book. I envision the remarriage of the church and the academy after all these centuries of a bitter divorce where the academy pleaded mental cruelty. The preacher as scholar may be the most important ministry of the local church in a secular, postmodern world where so many even question whether a smart person can believe in God.

Because this book resists the sermon that is based on interesting ideas and pop culture, it will probably earn easy dismissals. Some preachers will accuse me of being elitist and overly invested in scholarship. After all, I often make huge claims and I am not particularly gifted at qualifying those claims. One of the purposes of this book is to free those who preach from thinking that we must be overly attentive to what people think and how people will react to the toughness of the good news of Jesus Christ.

What I want to accomplish is to make preaching more capable of faithful proclamation and hearing of Scripture. Our failures in this regard are often related to our reluctance to make like Amos or one of the other prophets. Instead we parse our words, smooth out the tough spots, and take it as easy as possible on the listeners.

I am not making a case that preaching should be identical to the reading of a scholarly paper at a faculty convention. After all, academic language is an elite discipline that requires a certain set of skills that don't easily transfer to the pulpit. What bothers me is that preaching is too often treated as if it were not an academic discipline and as if it were a mere technique, a kind of following a recipe. As Plato insisted all those centuries ago in the Gorgias, there is a sort of bad rhetoric that is like cooking and it is mere quackery.

As to the charge that I am being elitist, I will let that stand. If attempting to clearly communicate the claims of Scripture from the pulpit makes me elitist, then I gladly bear the consequences of that charge. As Stanley Hauerwas notes, we have to be accountable to the "elite of the Church we call saints."[1]

My general observations about the state of preaching would be seriously remiss without mentioning the wealth of scholarship produced in the discipline of homiletics in the last seventy-five years. I have been deeply influenced by Carlyle Marney, Henry Mitchell, Gardner Taylor, Martin Luther King, Jr., John Claypool, William Sloan Coffin, Jr., David Buttrick, Fred Craddock, Walter Brueggemann, Barbara Brown Taylor, Richard Lischner, Thomas Long, and Richard Eslinger. There is a wealth of scholarship in homiletics but a dearth of its use Sunday after Sunday in many pulpits.

What I offer is scholarship as servant of the pulpit. Beginning with Saint Paul, the early church was dominated by scholarly preachers. The rather popular idea that the gospel is preached by country bumpkins with little or no education and is thus simple and easy is simply incapable of bearing the burden of proof in church history. The preacher/bishops of the first centuries were intellectual elites—trained as philosopher, rhetoricians, and theologians. The intellectual firepower of the church enabled the message to spread everywhere. I offer this history as an antidote to the suspicion that preachers often have of the academy and scholarship.

The problem with our preaching is that we have accommodated it to a secondary task in our weekly schedules and we have reduced it to a few stories or a laborious verse-by-verse teaching experience and our congregations, not knowing there is better fare, simply accept this as great preaching. The "sloth" that has gathered around the preaching experience has touched every aspect of the church's life. The seminary, charged with preparing students for pastoral ministry, requires one preaching course in a three-year Master of Divinity curriculum. This introduction to preaching doesn't have a chance of really impacting the would-be preachers. Churches routinely

---

1. Hauerwas, *Unleashing the Scripture*, 8.

INTRODUCTION

advertise for new preachers and it is rare not to see "excellent preacher" listed as one of the requirements sought by the pastoral search committee.

A sermon is a strange creation crafted from a strange world and an increasingly strange book—the Bible. I have studied, prepared, and preached sermons for more than four decades and I have discovered that there is a lot of "skirting around" the contributions of scholars (and that is a nice way of putting it) in many sermons. Sermons are sometimes about not trusting scholarship, or scholarship being too liberal, or scholarship not being of the Holy Spirit. On the other hand, other preachers might be afraid to share scholarly truth claims about scripture. Progressive preachers may preach without more than a passing reference to biblical texts (an add-on paragraph at the end of the sermon that is a sort of nod to a revered family member that now lives in a nursing home). For these preachers, biblical texts are no longer of any value. Leander Keck, forty years ago claimed that one set of preachers "misuse" the Bible and another set of preachers "disuse" the Bible.[2] More recently, Ellen Davis reflects on the tension between those who accuse preachers of no longer taking the Bible seriously as the guide for faith and life and those who believe the Bible is no longer fit to be the guide for faith and life. She laments that many clergy "no longer consider it necessary to speak in careful response to the biblical text" but have a different canon entirely—"the Atlantic Monthly or pop culture."[3]

Scholars usually contribute to sermons during the "originating moments" of the sermon. The narrator in the short story, "Hope of Zion," recalls the memory of a preacher's daughter about her father as a preacher. "In childhood Veronica had often spied on her father, the Reverend Douglas Fairfax, as he prepared and practiced his sermons. She remembered, with some anguish and embarrassment, how he would pore over his Bibles and clergyman's periodicals, searching for those certain passages that would make Mother's Day and home-coming messages meaningful to somebody's mother."[4] The preacher reads commentaries, essays, theology, ethics, and other books about the Bible. Some of that material becomes part of the sermon.

This volume places the contributions of scholars at the aftermath of the sermon—as part of an ongoing contribution and a new life to the sermon. Scholars who regularly listen to sermons are incredibly gracious and

---

2. Keck, *The Bible in the Pulpit*, 21.
3. Davis, *The Art of Reading Scripture*, 165.
4. Flowers, "Hope of Zion," in Susan Ketchin, *The Christ-Haunted Landscape*, 175.

INTRODUCTION

helpful. Their words to the preachers are encouraging words and not usually the kinds of necessary critiques offered to graduate students who are not writing clearly and not focused on a particular aspect of a topic. What scholars really think about the sermons they hear offers insights into the sheer difficulty of preaching and adds an additional level of contribution to the sermon that the church and her preachers can surely incorporate in the never-ending task of preaching better sermons. A diverse group of university professors and pastors have responded to the sermons in this volume: historians, ethicists, theologians, rhetoricians, philosophers, and pastors have engaged the sermons.

Each Sunday morning, I try to preach the perfect sermon, and each week I fail in that task. Sunday afternoon is often a tragedy and a terror as I unpack the sermon over lunch and my wife endures the recriminations that I impose on my effort to preach. This period of grief is necessary but can't be allowed to linger because Sunday will be back again real soon. As our son, Kirkland once suggested, "A sermon is like having a paper due every Sunday." And so it is. And oh what a glorious challenge. Gardner Taylor, in his Lyman Beecher lectures, referred to the Sunday morning sermon as the sweet agony.

Some of the contributors to this volume have only read the sermon manuscript that they received from me. The majority are scholars who listen to me preach Sunday after Sunday. On a deeply personal level, these responses are a way of "keeping my feet to the fire," and making sure that I am paying attention to the difficult work of speaking the gospel. I am reminded of the complexity of my task, a word-man in a world that has too many words and too many silent spaces. It will make me a better preacher and for that I will be eternally grateful.

My goal is for us to engage the terrifying good news of Jesus Christ the son of God. The response that preachers receive from sermons often doesn't survive beyond the casual "after-sermon" remarks at the church door on Sunday: "Nice sermon." "A bit long." "Wonderful job." Then there might be an email or two from people who were deeply moved by the sermon or a few emails from congregants who are upset about the truth claims of the sermon. These cryptic and well-meaning comments are usually the end of the sermon. It fades into memory and then ceases to exist entirely—lost in the never-never land of old sermons. While it is often said that some people never die, the reality here is that sermons die. Here is an attempt to produce several layers of conversation that will offer something other than casual phrases about sermons and engage the actual truth claims of the preacher in critical and meaningful ways. It is not an attempt to be elitist but to be honest. It is not an attempt to put down other conversation partners but to concentrate on scholars. This is part of my ongoing attempt to engage the church with the academy.

The loop that I am putting together involves me in conversation with biblical texts, with the scholarly interpreters of those texts, and then with scholars who hear and/or read my sermons. Your response then will be to the text itself and to the way I crafted a sermon on that text.

A sermon usually has a short shelf life. Like green bananas removed from the grocery bin, the sermon turns brown and mushy within a day or two. Once words of a sermon are spoken, they exist in isolation from the speaker and his/her meaning has no control over meanings others will ascribe to the sermon. After all, sermons are ubiquitous creatures and can mean at many levels and mean many things to different listeners.

Stanley Hauerwas says the sermon is an argument, but what else would a theologian who enjoys preaching say? You expect Stanley to use his prodigious argumentative skills to form the sermons he preaches. A cursory reading, if that is possible, of a Hauerwas sermon or two and the sermon as argument is nailed to the tree. John Claypool said the sermon was a conversation. He often spoke of the dialogue between the preacher and the congregation. There is much to commend the conversational model to our investigation of the sermon. What I attempt here is a combination model: sermon as argument and conversation. Walk into the back of any country store and plop down in a chair with a group of men. They have gathered in this spot every weekday morning from the beginning of time it seems. The conversations are rich, emotional, at times filled with laughter and at other times punctuated with the angry sounds of profanity. No one can cuss with rhythm like a Southern male in a dry goods store. The arguments are conversations and the snippets of argument are often decades old and are thrown into the fire like an old stick already burned on both ends. No one needs context or background. These men argue from experience formed on the anvil of deep relationships and harsh realities. Take a sermon and make it like that and see what happens.

Would it be possible to extend the shelf life of a sermon? Can a sermon survive in written form that is anywhere near the original impact of the sermon as delivered? After all, the difference between an auditory experience and a visual experience, the difference between reading and writing, the difference between hearing and thinking may be a great gulf that can't be crossed. Sermons almost never read as well as they preach. This is perhaps more obvious since the 1960's. Once written volumes of sermons crossed the Atlantic from British pulpits and became best sellers. Even the British accent seemed to be picked up in the reading of these sermons and the subsequent preaching of those sermons by American preachers. Even today, a preacher with a British accent has a leg up on those who preach only with a Midwestern twang. There's a certain allure, yes, sexiness, to English spoken by those for whom it has been the mother tongue for centuries.

One of the scholars I invited to participate in this project suggested to me that it was an impossible task. He pointed out the obvious disconnect between the purpose and the method of the project. "A sermon," he kindly reminded me, "is, potentially at least, an enormously dynamic occasion of communication where a speaker hopefully enables a parishioner to experience an intimate conversation with God in reference to ta text (I suppose as mediated by the Holy Spirit). It is time constrained and I am not sure it can ever be repeated except as a new communication.

"When the sermon becomes itself a printed or repeatable text, it takes on different properties. The review of such a text in the form of still another text falls into the realm of looking at the text's properties—what it has to say in a literary sense—in short, a discussion of its content and its rhetorical expression. I am not sure that creating such texts have much to do with making good sermons for most preachers."[5]

The objections thus stated are clear and true, but not necessarily the death knell for the project. Rhetorical scholars tell us that we live in the video-orality age. In other words, we have combined aspects of the ancient oral age of Homer with the video streaming age of the web. For preachers this is a bonanza of opportunities. For the sermon to be reproduced in a different setting and in a different form is not the barrier that it first seems to be. Since a sermon doesn't have an original meaning (it is a text after all), the sermon is capable of many different meanings and many different readings.

The ancient story tellers reproduced Homer's stories again and again and each new telling was a different version and yet the story remained the same. The shelf life has extended to this very day. We no longer hear the stories of Homer in any original sense, but in our reading, the imagined interactions we have with Homer and his stories remains potent and powerful.

---

5. Francis Miska, email correspondence, April 20, 2016.

INTRODUCTION

If the sermon is an ongoing conversation, then we are offering one way to make that happen. We are engaging in scholarly conversation. There is the sermon as delivered from the pulpit of First Baptist Church and now reproduced here in print. The respondents to these sermons often heard the sermon when I preached it and then read it in an email later that same Sunday. The experience for these scholars is deeper, richer, not because of any superiority of the sermon, but because they "received" the sermon in more than one venue: oral and literary. As William Trollinger has remarked to me on multiple occasions the sermon as preached is very different from the sermon read afterwards. If I were to preach this same sermon in a different church it would also be very different.

The audience shapes the sermons in dynamic ways that are unpredictable. For example, on a Sunday morning some years ago, I preached at the First United Methodist Church of Coral Gables, Florida. There were 3 services and I preached the same sermon all three times. The first sermon was at 8:30 in a small chapel to a group of 30 or so adults. The second sermon was in a family life center with 400 people, including children, bagels, coffee, orange juice and the ubiquitous PowerPoint screen. The third sermon was at 11:00 in the magnificent sanctuary. The three sermons, had they met on the street, would not have recognized one another. They would have been like elementary grade friends seeing one another for the first time in more than fifty years. There would have been faint memories and small connections, maybe even a family resemblance but other than that not much. Yet after a few awkward moments, as the conversation went here and there, in short bursts, and embarrassed laughter, there is an explosion of words and the memories come flooding back in auditory form. This is the sermon that I seek to preach—the single sermon that extends across time and space and engages more conversation partners, the one sermon that keeps alive the memory and becomes the word the world so desperately needs.

Preachers often live in isolation in reference to the sermons we preach. Unless there's controversy about a sermon, where is the serious, sustained, helpful pushback and critique that allows the preacher to sharpen skills and improve the sermon? I have attempted to provide a critical paradigm for preachers interested in improving their skill set. The sermons in this volume have been heard or read by an array of scholars from different disciplines. Each sermon is followed by one or more critiques. My purpose is to provide preachers with a way of critiquing sermons by studying how listeners/audiences receive sermons. There is a lot of difference between

INTRODUCTION

what the preacher thinks she has said and what the congregation heard the preacher say.

Communication depends far more on the listener than the speaker. Yet the preacher may not be that connected to the listeners. Sermons preached in such a monological fashion put the preacher in a homiletical cocoon and distanced from the people who actually determine whether or not the sermon delivered its promise of being a word from the Lord.

I take as a given that the usual feedback to the Sunday sermon is inadequate for the purposes of critical improvement by the preacher. "Good job, Reverend." "Nice sermon." "I enjoyed your sermon." "You really stepped on my toes this morning." In those moments at the end of the service, people quickly shake hands with the preacher, offer some brief words of encouragement, and head for lunch. If the preacher takes these offerings to mean that he is the best preacher in the nation, he has probably misread his congregation or his sermon or both.

The idea of exposing sermonic efforts to scholarly criticism may seem odd, but the potential for growth is too large to ignore. As I read the critiques of my own sermons, I was humbled by how the words were received and I was chastened by how much I had missed and how much I had failed to communicate clearly. The sermons would be different if I preached them again by incorporating the critiques that I received. It in this sense that I believe we have provided a workable methodology for preachers interested in improving as preachers.

The essays that follow each sermon both amplify and model the intellectual approach to preaching as a conversation that has been ongoing since the dawn of the art of Christian preaching. The essays are written from a variety of perspectives and the writers were under the expectation of writing critical responses. Agreement or disagreement, in this context, is beside the point. It is our hope that these sermons and responses may provide ongoing conversations with preachers and congregants within the church and the academy. Even a macro push in the direction of once again marrying the preaching event with the church and the academy will make of this work a fruitful and satisfying effort.

1

The Gospel Is Relevant
Mark 5:24–34

Let's begin with a simple claim: The gospel is relevant. Mark gives us a woman with long-term health issues! The gospel is relevant! She spent all that she had on doctors! The gospel is relevant! Jesus healed the woman of her long-term illness. The gospel is relevant! Quite the claim so let's take a look!

The woman with a twelve-year issue of blood might as well not exist in her time and especially not in ours. In a culture that worships the body, she doesn't count. Terry Eaglton says the body is the greatest fetish of all. Sarah Coakley argues that we are putting our trust in the body and our souls are shriveling. The body, worshiped as god, turns out to have a short shelf life and to be constantly in need of repair, routine maintenance that costs more per hour than a tune-up for a Mercedes, replacement parts, and plastic surgery. And yet we all know what happens to bodies. So this woman's body is ravaged by disease. Her ability to be attractive has been destroyed by years of living in the street, homeless and penniless. She is enslaved by the expected performances of the culture that is the drama of life in the first century. This story matters because this one woman is about to smash to bits centuries of abuse of people as a category of the unclean. The paradigm of what counted as "unclean" is going down. What has felt like predestination is about to be unmasked by an act of free will. Evicted from her home, fired from her job, refused service at restaurants, uncared for by anyone, she is in solitary confinement. One rule: No Touching. Elisabeth Kubler-Ross, in the beautiful Highland Country of Virginia, tried to establish a hospice for children with AIDS. Her neighbors rose in protest. They would not let her go forward. They were afraid. We often act out our fears based on misinformation and then multiply the tragedy by saying that we are just doing what God told us to do.

No one can blame parents for protecting their children. In Mary Gordon's *Men and Angels* one woman asks another, "What do you think having children does to your moral life?"[1] The other woman says, "When you're a mother you think with your claws."[2] I get that and I even like it, but we can be overprotective when we continue to insist that some group is going to destroy family life in America.

Scripture was not written in stone! As far as I can tell, the only Scripture ever written on stone was the Ten Commandments and they didn't make it down the mountain in one piece. Scripture is written on the heart and thus it has living, compassionate meanings that you can't wring from a stone. Stone-cold hearts, accusatory fingers wrapped around stone-formed Scriptures. Such monstrous Christianity may turn you, like Medusa, to stone. Only idols/false gods are made of stone. Our God is not a god of stone and the Word of our God is not a word of stone. The boundary keepers who try to keep everyone in their designated place think they are following scared Scripture but may only be worshiping sacred cows. It is not an uncommon problem for God's children. While waiting for the word of God to come down Mt. Sinai they built a golden calf and worshiped it.

Of all things, on his way to help an important male authority figure with his sick 12-year-old daughter Jesus stops to help a nameless woman. Jarius, the male leader is a synagogue official; she is excluded from the religious community. As leader of the synagogue he probably wrote the decree that expelled her from the synagogue. It would have happened 12 years ago. Joel Marcus suggests the "twelve" is the key word that caused Mark to tie the stories of Jarius and the woman with the issue of blood together.[3] So at the time that he celebrated the gift of life in a beautiful new daughter, he gives a virtual death sentence to a woman condemned as unclean. Jairus has a family and a large household; she is alone in the world. He is rich; she

---

1. Gordon, Men and Angels, loc. 3311, (Location will refer to Kindle editions of books.).

2. Ibid, loc. 3320.

3. Joel Marcus, *The Gospel of Mark*, 357.

is impoverished by payment of doctors' fees. He was somebody: Ruler of the synagogue. She was nobody.

Listen for a moment to the woman. Her lips are moving as she engages in self-conversation. Mark is not an omnipotent narrator in this story. He can't read the minds and motivations of the characters in his story. This may be an eye-witness account, a testimony the woman later offered to Mark. "She was saying to herself" means muttering in a half-crazed, numb condition. We all talk to ourselves, especially when desperate or in danger. Self-talk can be a necessary survival technique. But we need more than self-talk. Like this woman, we need to reach out to the healing power of Jesus for support.

Look at her! She is so horrendous our eyes dart away as if one of those ads depicting a skeletal, starving child in Ethiopia is on the screen. Mark piles up seven consecutive participles and they roll off the tongue in a slow beat like a funeral dirge: And a woman being in a flow of blood for twelve years, and having endured many treatments from many doctors, and having spent all her money on them and not having benefited at all but rather having gotten worse, having heard about Jesus and having come behind him in the crowd, touched his garment. Then the word "touched" explodes into the room. Action now!

She had heard about Jesus, and came up behind him in the crowd and touched his cloak, for she said, "If I but touch his clothes, I will be made well." This woman has some odd beliefs. Don't we all? Yet, in spite of her inadequate beliefs, she is healed. Isn't it amazing how little faith is required for a miracle? I wonder why we are so insistent that people have more faith and more doctrinal purity. Why can't we quit fussing and get on with the faithfulness? Here's a faith that has heard about Jesus, and just to add a bit of flavor she has some magical notions and some superstition. She believes she must come into physical contact in order to be cured by him. Faith is always a mixed bag even if you are pretty certain about well, everything.

Read the medical chart: [29]Immediately her hemorrhage stopped; and she felt in her body that she was healed of her disease. Now look at her again! Can you guess why her chin is lifted? "Why does she breathe as if to show exactly how it's done? Why should both her shoulders, usually quite bent, brace so square right now?"[4] She is the vanguard of a new world for women and wherever women are still treated as less than equal she is there as the standard bearer. She is guarding the world for women! And it

4. Gurganus, *White People*, 138.

all started with a touch—a rebellious touch in defiance of the boundary keepers.

But immediately Jesus, knowing in himself that power had gone out of him, turned in the crowd and said, "Who touched my clothes?" Jesus sensed that power had gone out from him. There is a flow of power that is so free, so open to the world of agony and suffering, that when Jesus is touched, his power responds faster than a Japanese super train. Get close to Jesus and touch him and the power is unleashed. There can't be a better first step for a troubled soul to take. You will touch the source of all the creative energy in the universe, the energy God unleashed billions of years ago for our well-being and salvation. All this energy continues unabated—the goodness of God still looking for places to plug in and make a difference. This is surely the good news the world is dying to hear. Need is the only criteria not value or worth or status.

"Who touched me?" The question is rhetorical and doesn't suggest a lack of knowledge. In the Greek text it reads that Jesus "continued to look around to see her who had done this." Jesus sensed she was unclean, desperate. He knew and yet the power, without prejudice, without checking to see if this person was on the approved list, went out. Woosh! The power is released to meet the need.

The old authority figures, the people who make it their business to scare us about violating their stone rules, make it their business to say this unclean woman's touch will destroy the power of Jesus' healing. Well, it's time to straighten up and fly right! The power of Jesus is greater than the lies of the boundary keepers. "Instead of uncleanness passing from the woman to Jesus, healing power flows from Jesus to the woman." The power of uncleanness turns out to be a human, rhetorical construction, a human judgment that has no power except that granted by a willing majority to treat people as unclean. The power of Jesus always overcomes the power of a people depending on words written in stone.

"But Jesus continued looking around to see the woman who had done this." Jesus concentrates on the woman whose need has caused her to reach out to him. The focus of Jesus is on the woman not on the words written in stone that had condemned her. The self-awareness of the woman and of Jesus is just remarkable. "She knew in her body." "Jesus, knowing in himself that power had gone out of him." What a deep connection—a visceral, human, fleshly connection between a woman's need and a Savior's power.

Now, hear the good news: [33]"Daughter, your faith has made you well; go in peace, and be healed of your disease." What does this mean for us? Our imperfect, mixed-up, notions of faith can bring forth the healing power of Jesus. When need reaches out to us, we can direct the flow of Jesus' power, grace, and mercy in their direction. Instead of cold stone we can be a people of the heart to meet all this human need. The gospel is relevant!

Response
The Gospel Is Relevant

____ Steve Harmon ____

THE GOSPEL IS INDEED relevant, as Rodney Kennedy claims at the outset of this sermon. If it is not relevant, it is not the Gospel, for the Gospel is nothing other than God's act of relating good news about God and about humanity to human recipients of this news who, lacking this good news, have assumptions about God and themselves that leave them with less than a meaningful, hopeful, and wholesome existence. The Gospel is relevant because it gives people what they need - not necessarily what they want, and whether or not they realize they need it. We could easily say the same things about the nature of divine revelation, for this good news about God and humanity is what God discloses in God's work of revelation. The Gospel is revelant because of the good news it reveals about God and ourselves.

It seems clear to me that Rodney shares this theological understanding of the revelatory nature of the Gospel and its relevance. He, the preacher, is not the one who lends relevance to the Gospel through his preaching of this Gospel story. The Gospel possesses its text by exploring further the revelatory function of the Gospel stories in general and this Gospel story in particular. A few years ago I served as interim pastor of a church during a Markan year in the lectionary. I decided to make the guiding principle of a church-year-long series of sermons based on the lectionary readings from Mark the church's traditional understanding of the incarnate Christ as fully divine and fully human, and therefore as the one who both reveals who God is and as the one who reveals who God intends us to be—in other words, as the one who preaches the relevant good news about God and humanity. In these sermons I directed two questions to each story about Jesus: (1) What does this story teach us about who God is?, and (2) What does this story teach us about who we are and who we ought to be? Though my sermons were probably not as eloquently expressed and skillfully communicated as Rodney's, I think they worked in terms of helping hearers see the relevance of the good news God makes known in Jesus Christ.

In my reading of the Markan narrative through the lenses of the church's traditional teaching that the incarnate Christ is both fully divine and fully human, I was also drawing upon James Wm. McClendon, Jr.'s critique of the "two natures" conceptual language with which the patristic church influentially expressed this teaching about Jesus, most definitively at the Council of Chalcedon in AD 451. McClendon proposed as a replacement for the "two natures" Christology a "two-narrative Christology."[1] In this account, one's identity is located not in one's classification according to abstract categories of "natures," divine or human. Rather, one's identity is nothing other than one's story. A person's story—in its totality and in its particularity—is the thickest possible description one can offer of a person's identity.[2] For the incarnate Christ, this narrative identity is both twofold and singular. In my recent book on Baptist Identity and the Ecumenical Future, in which I drew on McClendon's "two-narrative" Christology to propose a narrative-Christological approach to ecclesiology, I attempted to summarize what McClendon proposes in my own words, intentionally echoing the two-natures-in-one-person template of the Chalcedonian Definition:

The story of Christ fully encompasses and discloses the story of the Triune God, which is God's identity. At the same time the story of Christ fully encompasses and discloses the story of humanity, which is our

---

1. McClendon, *Doctrine*, 263–79.

2. Cf. F. Michael McLain, "Narrative Interpretation and the Problem of Double Agency," in *Divine Action: Studies Inspired by the Philosophical Theology of Austin Farrer*, ed. Brian Hebblethwaite and Edward Henderson (Edinburgh: T&T Clark, 1990), 143: "If God is an agent who acts in the world so as to disclose divine character and purpose, then narrative is the appropriate form in which to render God's identity." Daniel L. Migliore cites McLain in connection with his own observations on the connection between narrative, identity, and revelation: "[O]ur identity as persons is often rendered in narrative form. If this is true of our self-disclosure to each other, by analogy it is also true of the self-disclosure of God" (Migliore, *Faith Seeking Understanding: An Introduction to Christian Theology*, 2nd ed. [Grand Rapids, Mich.: William B. Eerdmans, 2004], 37).

identity. Yet these two distinguishable stories, these two identities, are in Jesus Christ one indivisible narrative identity.[3]

This is how McClendon himself summarized his proposal:

> Therefore we have these two stories, of divine self-expense and human investment, of God reaching to people even before people reach to God, of a God who gives in order to be able to receive, and a humanity that receives so that it shall be able to give. Together, they constitute the biblical story in its fullness. *And now the capstone word is this: these two stories are at last indivisibly one.* We can separate them for analysis, but we cannot divide them; there is but one story there to be told. Finally, this story becomes gospel, becomes good news, when we discover that it is our own.[4]

Notwithstanding McClendon's declaration that "two-natures Christology has had its day, and we need not return to it,"[5] I see his two-narrative alternative not as a replacement for Chalcedon but as an extension and enrichment of it. McClendon's Christology teases out additional implications of the incarnation beyond what could be expressed within the constraints of the Chalcedonian categories by re-reading the Council's insights in light of a new set of questions and categories that belong to a context other than the Hellenism of late antiquity—namely, the West after modernity. McClendon's qualifications regarding the relation of the two narratives to each other actually correspond to those of the Chalcedonian Definition: the two narrative identities may be separated for analysis ("without confusion"), but they cannot be divided ("without division or separation").

I did not tell the congregation about McClendon and his "two-narrative" Christology while I was their interim pastor, but it was the theological framework presupposed in preparing and preaching each of those sermons. It enabled me, and I hope the congregation as well, to see Mark's story about Jesus both as the story that defines who God is and how acts in relation to us and as the story that defines who we really are and who we should seek to be as followers of Jesus.

Rodney's sermon on Jesus' healing of the woman with an issue of blood gives attention to who God is and who we are and ought to be. The God portrayed in this sermon "is not a god of stone"—not a god who would insist on "boundary keeping." What enables Rodney to say this about God

---

3. Harmon, *Baptist Identity and the Ecumenical Future*, 233.
4. McClendon, *Doctrine*, 276–77.
5. Ibid, 276.

is what Jesus does in transcending boundaries in this story: Jesus crosses boundaries that exclude from religious community in order to make this woman whole, included by the boundary-transcending God. Rodney does not explicitly say that because Jesus crosses boundaries created by people who imagine God to be a boundary-keeping god, but that seems to be the clear implication of his sermon. I trust that those who heard it would have made the connection without being prompted—but now and then it doesn't hurt to make such things so clear they can't be missed.

This story about Jesus also tells us the truth about the human story, our story—it both exposes our failures to be who God created us to be and narrates in advance the story that should be embodied by our lives, and can yet be through Christ's transformative work of making his story ours in actuality. If Jesus in this story is not about boundary-keeping, then neither should that be our focus. If Jesus in this story goes about transcending the boundaries created by people who imagine God to be a boundary-keeping god, then our task is to identify such boundaries and not only to transcend them ourselves but to call for their erasure in our society. It seems clear that Rodney hopes this story would have those effects on his hearers, and I trust that those who had ears to hear heard that implication of the story and hopefully heeded it. Again, now and then it doesn't hurt to make it unmistakably clear how we ought to live differently in light of what we've heard. But there's more than one way to do that, and one very effective way to gesture toward what it might mean to embody the biblical story is to point to real people beyond the biblical text who have done just that.[6] Rodney does this early in his sermon: he makes reference to Elisabeth Kübler-Ross' efforts to establish a hospice for children with HIV and contrasts this contemporary embodiment of the boundary-transcending story of Jesus and contrasts it with the boundary-keeping response of her neighbors. Having established early in the sermon what it means for people to embody the story Jesus sets out for us as the story that ought to be ours, it isn't necessary for Rodney to keep reiterating the application; he can focus on offering a compelling re-telling of this story of Jesus' transcending of boundaries, and what his hearers should be thinking along the way toward the conclusion of the sermon is "a person besides Jesus has done this, and therefore we can and should, too."

6. Cf. Hays and Davis, "Beyond Criticism: Learning to Read the Bible Again," *Christian Century* 121, no. 8 (April 20, 2004): 23–27, who include this among the "theses on interpreting Scripture" they propose: "7. The saints of the church provide guidance in how to interpret and perform Scripture" (26).

As I read this sermon, preached originally in May 2015, I kept thinking about all the ways our contemporary culture, in the United States and more broadly in the Western world, has quickly become even more concerned with boundary-keeping than it was in May 2015—and it was certainly marking our culture then. It made me think of our treatment of immigrants, of refugees, of the racial "other," of those whose sexual identities are "other." It made me connect all this with the boundary-transcending God whose story is told by the story of Jesus, and it reminded me that the boundary-transcending story of Jesus should become more and more my own story. I pray that it does, and I'm grateful to Rodney for writing and preaching a sermon that made this my prayer. The Gospel is relevant, indeed.

2

God Is Good!
Mark 4:1–32

THIS IS A SERMON about God and God's goodness. The church should trust the goodness of the Lord! God is good! God is good! God is good all the time!

Mark 4 is about God's goodness wrapped in first century farming practices. Mark 4 opens with the parable of the farmer slinging seed all over the place. Mark adds an allegorical interpretation of the parable.[1] The interpreter is obsessed with the dirt and the weeds and the thorns and the rocks. He gives four times as much attention to the bad news as he does the good news. About average. Only one verse is given over to the actual theme of the parable: "And these are the seeds sown in the good earth: they who hear the word and accept it and bear fruit, thirtyfold, sixtyfold, and a hundredfold."

Some of us have imbibed a bad batch of religion that claims the dirt, the soil, and the fleshly are somehow wicked and evil. But mark this down: The Bible has a different opinion about dirt. In Mark 4 it is called "good soil." In Genesis 1 everything earthly is called good. God saw to it that it was all good. And God created humankind from the dirt. St. Augustine wrote, "So it became obvious to me that all that God has made is good, and that there are no substances whatsoever that were not made by [God]. And because [God] did not make them all equal, each single thing is good and

---

1. Marcus, *Mark 1–8*, 301.

collectively they are very good, for our God made his whole creation very good."[2]

Jesus says, "From the soil, there's going to be a harvest." Promised by God. Guaranteed by the Son. Brought by the power of the Holy Spirit. Thirty, sixty, a hundred times—there's going to be a harvest. God is going to take our foolish, inept throwing out of seeds and turn them into victory. There's a goodness that encircles the universe, a mighty defense shield that can't be penetrated by terrorism, hatred, meanness, skepticism, doubt, war, or nuclear holocaust. God is good![3]

"The kingdom of God", Jesus says, "is like a mustard seed." A mustard seed was the biblical kudzu or honeysuckle. One plant was there today and tomorrow there were six and a month later there were 6,000. You couldn't beat it back, cut it back, or burn it off. There's no stopping it once you plant it.

There's a song about two good old boys living on a farm and they discover this sort of weed that they put in their corn cob pipes and smoke. "Take a trip and never leave the farm."

As long as we have a sack of seeds, there's nothing the world can do to keep us from spreading the good news. The good news is like the mustard plant. Indestructible, relentless, unhindered. Here's the deal! The kingdom is a "mustard plant" that attracts all kinds of birds, including strange ones and we are not in charge of its meanings. Oh how wonderful to know that we have received such a powerful kingdom.

Goodness, good news, and God cannot be separated in the life of Jesus. They are the same. "Showing" or "picturing" is the heart of the matter. Goodness shouldn't be shy and reluctant among God's people. We need to be out there spreading the goodness. But we are a reticent bunch aren't we? Will Campbell once conceded to his imaginary African-American confessor, T. J., "You know, sometimes I get tired of working behind the scenes." T. J. responds, "Yeah, I guess it does get kind of crowded back there sometimes."

There is a cosmic force for goodness in this universe and nothing can defeat it. As David Bentley Hart, in *The Doors of the Sea* puts it, "Knowledge central to the gospel: the knowledge of the evil of death, its intrinsic falsity, its unjust dominion over the world, its ultimate nullity; the knowledge that God is not pleased or nourished by our deaths, that he is not the secret architect of evil, that he is the conqueror of hell, that he has condemned

---

2. Augustine, *Confessions*, 148, 7.12.
3. Marcus, *Mark 1–8*, 293.

all these things by the power of the cross; the knowledge that God is life and light and infinite love, and that the path that leads through nature and history to his Kingdom does not simply follow contours of either.[4] Darkness can't smother goodness. Evil can't defeat goodness. Death can't destroy goodness. "God is light and in him there is no darkness at all: (I John 1:5). Remember the game rock, paper, and scissors. "Rock smashes scissors; paper covers rock; scissors cut paper. There is a hilarious expansion of this game in multiple episodes of *The Big Bang Theory*: Sheldon explains the rules to Penny and Barry Kripke: Scissors cut Paper / Paper covers Rock / Rock crushes Lizard / Lizard poisons Spock / Spock smashes Scissors / Scissors decapitates Lizard / Lizard eats Paper / Paper disproves Spock / Spock vaporizes Rock / (and as it always has) Rock crushes scissors.

Goodness crushes evil. We are called by God to confront evil and respond to it with goodness. What do you suppose that looks like for Christians to respond to everything with goodness? What if our default response should be goodness? Try an example: If an ultra-Orthodox Jew refuses to sit next to a woman on an airplane, and you are that woman what would you do? You have every right to keep your seat. Would it be the Christian thing to do that you would respect his religious conviction by practicing your Christian conviction to turn the other cheek and to return his strangeness with your goodness? Isn't there something off key about Christians yammering about rights when we are slaves of Jesus? One way to tell that your faith has become more American than Christian is if you are always going on to doomsday about your rights. It feels like being trapped in a Flannery O'Connor story where hell is being one of those people in Georgia who has to sit and listen to your mother talk to you all day and all night, and you're ugly and peg-legged and must hear your mother go on about how dancing will send you to hell and stay out of the pool hall and all that degradation and manifold iniquity till doomsday.

Well, the way of Jesus was to be the servant.[5] Will Campbell put the following conjecture in T. J.'s mouth: "When you think about it there's something pretty selfish about trying so hard to get my rights. Maybe the Christian thing to be doing is to be handing over the rights I already have. Jesus said don't resist evil or persecution. Said if you take away my sweater to give you my coat. I'm telling you that as I read the Book, Brother Jesus is asking us to give up power, not get more. All those white cats under the

---

4. Hart, *The Doors of the Sea*, 101.
5. Campbell, "Whose Freedom?"

big steeple churches, yeah they got power to give up. They got influence. And what's it good for? Go tell'em to get rid of some of their power and influence. And when white folks drop their power, I'll tell mine to let it lie where it fell. Not to pick it up. Cause if they do they're in a peck of trouble."[6] So if a Christian baker refuses to make a wedding cake for a gay couple, wouldn't it be Christian to find another baker rather than insisting on legal rights and filing suit? I Corinthians 6:1–6 says, "When any of you has a grievance against another, do you dare to take it to court before the unrighteous, instead of taking it before the saints? [2]Do you not know that the saints will judge the world? And if the world is to be judged by you, are you incompetent to try trivial cases? [3]Do you not know that we are to judge angels—to say nothing of ordinary matters? [4]If you have ordinary cases, then, do you appoint as judges those who have no standing in the church? [5]I say this to your shame. Can it be that there is no one among you wise enough to decide between one believer and another, [6]but a believer goes to court against a believer—and before unbelievers at that?"

Now that we have the power, are we going to use it against the conservative Christians and if so, why? In Genesis, there's a baker who offended the king and the king hanged the baker. That's not Christian.

We think that goodness derives from power, but goodness is not concerned with power. Still, we are engaged in typical power battles. How often do we want our goodness to come from our power? Who among us would be willing to put down the power we have? Put down your power and then let goodness flow like honey from the rock. Jesus was offered all the power in the world by Satan and even as Satan tried to fit him with the purple robe of all that power, Jesus put it off like a country boy shucking corn. Instead of putting down one another, put down condescending and patronizing ways. Preachers face a lot of patronizing in the South. "You wouldn't believe our little preacher, he is the cutest thing, all those pretty curls. He is a ball of fire. He talks about our kids going to go to school with "blacks". He is a card, you know. He is a character; you know he is sort of our mascot. We love him and won't pay any attention to him. We don't believe all that, but it is nice to have the only preacher in town with a real Ph.D." The good people accepted the pride and power that came from having an educated pastor but completely rejected the preacher's message. Who among us would practice some gospel and put down our power? I think we are continually confusing power with goodness. Liberals often mistake secular altruism for God's

---

6. Campbell and Goode, *Crashing the Idols*, 95–97.

goodness. The question is not how much power do we have, but how much goodness will we practice? If you want to be a difference maker in this world, don't seek the power but triple-down on goodness, acts of goodness, practices of goodness, sheer, complete, unexpected, second mile goodness.

We need to trust the gospel to do its work. Will Campbell wrote to the National Council of Churches' General Board of Social Concerns: "We just can't quite trust the power of the Gospel message. There just must be something we can add, some gimmick, some technique, some strategy. Just this once I wanted to rely only upon this [the gospel] and if it wasn't enough then let it not be enough. I am more and more convinced that it is enough if our witness to it is faithful."[7]

As Christians we are to live lives spreading the goodness of God. How much sheer goodness are we willing to show and share in this city?

To learn to follow Jesus is the training necessary to become goodness. There may be nothing less Christian than insisting on our rights and using our power to get our way. To learn to live without rights, without certainty, without power, without protection, and without possessions is to follow Jesus. To trust the harvest of goodness is to trust the goodness of God. God is good! God is good! God is good all the time!

---

7. Ibid, *Crashing the Idols*, 27.

Response

God Is Good!

———— Herbie Miller ————

Rodney Kennedy's sermon is unsettling in the way all good sermons should be. He draws his audience into the strange world of the text. He creates a rhetorical event in which their theological convictions can be interrogated. And he proclaims the good news in a way that is not a recycling of platitudes. As good as his sermon is, Kennedy leaves unanswered a pertinent question that can leave readers wondering about the implications of his message for communities who have experienced historic oppression and marginalization.

The Strange World of Mark 4

In choosing to preach from Mark 4, Kennedy uses the parables of the sower and the mustard seed to illustrate God's goodness. To American readers well-schooled in the capitalist economics of scarcity, the farming practices of Mark's sower probably seem unintelligible: How careless it is to knowingly throw one's seed on inhospitable soil? Why didn't the farmer have a strategic plan for planting his crops? Such farming practices lack strategy at best, and at worst are simply wasteful. The parable, however, is for Kennedy an illustration of how God transforms our haphazard efforts to spread the good news of Jesus Christ into an abundant harvest. We may be "inept," as Kennedy notes, in our throwing of the seeds; but God mysteriously transforms our inept actions into victory. Following his discussion of the sower, Kennedy reminds his readers of Mark's mustard seed, which Kennedy calls "indestructible, relentless, unhindered"—all adjectives he will use to describe the good news.

Kennedy uses the parables to preach on the themes of grace and providence, but without coming right out and saying he is talking about these two doctrines. For Kennedy, human actors proclaim and embody the good news, but they are not the primary subjects *doing* the acting. They are secondary subjects whose efforts are conscripted into the providential action of God—the primary subject—in the world. This theological move enables Kennedy to lift a burden off his hearers' shoulders, which is the feeling that the success or failure of the Kingdom of God depends on their human effort. While individual Christians are responsible for practicing goodness in the world, God is the One who sees to it that the seed of goodness grows. And once that good news starts to grow, it will be like the mustard seed—indefatigable.

A Surprising Interrogation of Progressive Christianity

In articulating this grace-filled and counter-cultural message of goodness, Kennedy has created a rhetorical space in which he can challenge his audience's assumptions about the issue of rights. At the end of his sermon, Kennedy remarks that "there may be nothing less Christian than insisting on our rights and using our power to get our way." Rather than clinging to their rights, Kennedy wants his readers to give them up. He challenges his audience to consider the possibility that their militant obsession with protecting their private rights hinders their Christian witness.

Surprisingly, Kennedy's two examples do not take aim at conservative Christians, who are often concerned with the issue of religious liberty as it relates to such things as the legality of Nativity scenes or the Ten Commandments on government property. Instead, he seems to be challenging progressive Christians to consider the ways in which they, too, have become myopically focused on their personal rights at the expense of their Christian witness. The first example is about a woman on an airplane seated next to an Orthodox Jewish man; her seatmate cannot sit beside her because of his religious strictures. The second is about a gay couple that has been refused service by a baker because of his or her unwillingness to serve a homosexual couple. To use Kennedy's language, what would be "the Christian thing to do?" For the woman to remain in her seat? For the gay couple to file a lawsuit? While we can't know for sure, presumably progressive Christians would encourage the woman to stay in her seat and the gay couple to use the legal system to receive service from the baker. Kennedy, though, wants to challenge the woman and the gay couple, if they are Christians, to give away their rights to persons who hold social and theological views they deplore.

And in so doing, Kennedy touches a nerve. His realistic examples confront readers with a troubling question: Is it appropriate for Christians to ask other Christians who have been historically marginalized and oppressed to abnegate their rights in the name of Christ? Such a conversation seems unthinkable for some given the enduring reality of discrimination based on gender and sexual orientation in America and across the globe (and this is not to mention race, which did not factor into Kennedy's examples). Nevertheless, Kennedy wants us to talk.

An Uncomfortable Proclamation of the Gospel

Kennedy is fully aware that he has kicked a hornet's nest. He knows that a person is able to abnegate his or her rights only when they have those rights to begin with. He also seems to know that it is much easier for a person with an excess of social and legal privilege to spout off about giving away their rights. In the heart of his sermon, when he gives the examples of the woman on the airplane and the gay couple refused service, Kennedy offers two anecdotes from the writings of Will Campbell, the twentieth century white Christian who worked for racial justice in the American South. In the examples, Campbell is talking with his "imaginary African-American confessor, T.J.," who in the second quote states bluntly, "when white folks drop their power, I'll tell mine to let it lie where it fell. Not to pick it up. Cause if they do they're in a peck of trouble." Kennedy's sermon is an invitation into an uncomfortable theological discussion about the relationship between proclaiming/practicing the good news on the one hand, and having painful conversations about rights and privilege on the other.

Homiletic Suggestions

As a reader, I believe Kennedy's sermon could be stronger by giving his audience direction about what to do with the message he has just preached. He invites Christians "to learn to live without rights . . . without power . . . without protection." What his audience needs, following that admonition, is help knowing what it implies for their day-to-day lives. The virtue of prudence, I contend, is what they need to know if/when/how one should live without these things in their particular contexts. The reader would have benefited from an example of when it is appropriate to assert, rather than abnegate, one's rights. Kennedy has shocked us into knowing that we need prudence, but he doesn't equip us with the skills necessary to live a life that makes his admonition workable. Kennedy could have been more explicit here. In his concluding paragraph he says, "to learn to follow Jesus is the training necessary to become goodness," which is a statement that reveals that he understands the centrality of discipleship, formation, and virtue for the Christian life.

Conclusion

As it stands, Kennedy's sermon succeeds in its succinct and effective proclamation of the gospel of Jesus Christ, which in this context is to challenge Christians to know that there are times when for the sake of sowing the good news they will need to give away their rights. However, it fails to provide the audience with the tools (the virtue of prudence) needed to contextualize the admonition to live without rights. For example, should readers who have experienced oppression and marginalization because of their gender or sexual orientation stop fighting for their rights and acquiesce to social attitudes and laws that prevent their full human flourishing? While this author is virtually certain that Kennedy would *not* want this, one could finish his sermon and reasonably conclude that it is.

3

Excel in Generosity
II Corinthians 9

PAUL IS HITTING UP his congregation for a donation. It's a big deal, but there's something here more important than the money. We know that money is not everything but we should repeat the idea because it is easy to lose sight of the reality. Money is not everything. Money has ethical implications. Money is neither all good nor all bad. We know we can't take it with us but that is not the "drop dead" argument for having nothing to do with money. All of us are embedded in the culture of money. In the fabric of everyday life, money touches everything, even our sense of time. We say, "Time is money." Money matters. To talk about humans without talking about money is like talking about bees and not bringing up honey. I am not here for your money; the sermon is about bigger, more important principles.

Then without catching his breath Paul pushes even harder and asks the church to excel in everything. Paul wants more than money. The money will not matter if the heart is not right. Paul says for us to excel in generosity, but see how easily we can flip that to excelling in the opposite of generosity—a spirit of judgmentalism. If we are not careful we will not have glad and generous hearts. Young people in America say that Christians are judgmental and hypocritical and they have quit the place and many of them are struggling to even believe in God. If we are going to win them back, a generous spirit would be a good starting point.

We can strive for the kind of excellence that is life robbing. John Brueggemann, in *Rich, Free, and Miserable: The Failure of Success in America* says, "In one large study, the main wish children expressed in terms of how their families could be different was for their parents to be less stressed and less tired . . . ."[1] Children are not happy living in a money-obsessed culture. We often think money will buy happiness, but not for our children. Have you seen the ad where the children are begging parents to take vacations: Kids talk about the paid vacation days people don't take during the year. "We've heard that over 400,000,000 vacation days go unused every year. That's the stupidest thing I ever heard. They're paid vacation days. If you guys agreed to travel more we'll all do better in school. We'll have a better understanding of other cultures. I will learn to *parlez français*. Oui oui. We're not asking for much. We just want one more day. One more day! Because one more day is priceless."

God and money are always mixed together. We may love God but we also need money. Jesus said it flat out: You cannot love God and money, but Jesus or no Jesus, we love both. Aviad Kleinberg, in *Seven Deadly Sins*, says that the church itself is possessed by possessions. We are all up to our steeples in God and money. It is not an accident that the Catholic Church has the Vatican Bank. God and Money.

We wage unending battle between two very different economies. The Bible calls it the economy of Mammon and the economy of Manna. We are up to our portfolios in this same battle. I know the CEO of Goldman and Sachs once said "We are doing God's work," but there is a world of difference between the church and Wall Street. Mammon is a sneaky god. It even dresses up and comes to church. Sitting in church, singing "How Great Thou Art," you can be thinking about your investments; saying your prayers, you can be wondering when you will get paid; asking God for forgiveness, you may be anxious about your debts. While saying the Lord's Prayer, another message will play in your mind: There must be more money!

Let me show you a biblical example from the book of Amos: "When will the new moon be over so that we may sell grain; and the Sabbath so that we may offer wheat for sale?"[2] The overwhelming desire for money can reduce even Sabbath—the anti-currency of culture—to a mere nuisance.

I'm not asking you to be unproductive. That would be counter-productive. Listen, some religious ideas will mess you up as badly as Mammon.

---

1. Brueggemann, *Rich, Free and Miserable*, 87.
2. Amos 8:5, *NRSV*.

At the church in Thessalonica, some Christians got the idea that since Jesus was coming back any day now, they should quit their jobs and sit around waiting for the rapture. Paul moves quickly to squash the danger: "Anyone unwilling to work should not eat. ¹¹For we hear that some of you are living in idleness, mere busybodies, not doing any work." Let me repeat: I am not suggesting that you become unproductive, lazy, and worthless.

So St. Paul disrupts to offer an alternative economy based on generosity: "The one who had much did not have too much, and the one who had little did not have too little." He's quoting Exodus 16 where God provides manna for the children of Israel: "This is what the Lord has commanded: 'Gather as much of it as each of you needs, according to the number of persons, all providing for those in their own tents.' The Israelites did so, some gathering more, some less."

Now add this verse from Acts 2: "All who believed were together and had all things in common; ⁴⁵they would sell their possessions and goods and distribute the proceeds to all, as any had need."[3] And Acts 4: "Now the whole group of those who believed were of one heart and soul, and no one claimed private ownership of any possessions, but everything they owned was held in common. With great power the apostles gave their testimony to the resurrection of the Lord Jesus. There was not a needy person among them, for as many as owned lands or houses sold them and brought the proceeds of what was sold, and it was distributed to each as any had need."[4] This passage suggests that the resurrection changes the way we think about economics. It also chips away at the notion of private property. As the children of John loc.e, we don't care much for "no one claimed private ownership of any possessions." Locke argued that we have inalienable rights and one of these inalienable rights is the right to private property. The American dream is to own property, own a house, but for Christians private property is not everything.

This is a good example of how American Christians are not serious about all of the Bible. It's funny about those who are so sure that we should always follow the straight, plain meaning of the Bible have no interest in the economy of Manna. My cousin Boudreaux says this business about having everything in common in downright un-American.

You know what the problem is don't you? These stories disrupt because they sound like—go ahead say it out loud—this business of selling

---

3. Acts 2:44–47, NRSV.
4. Acts 4:32–35, NRSV.

everything and having stuff in common—sounds like—socialism. It may feel like cognitive dissonance to many American Christians, but the gospel is not America-friendly or capitalist-friendly.

What Paul calls generosity the world calls socialism. The accusation of socialism lies always on the lips of Americans. Social is such a good word. I love church socials. I am a social creature. I will soon be eligible for Social Security. I try to have as much social capital as possible. Social networking is an important part of my life. The gospel is social. Say the words "social gospel" and some people see red. When the Baptist leader Walter Rauschenbusch developed the "social gospel," American Christians went crazy. Walter died in 1918 and he is still the most criticized Baptist in the world. Washington Gladden, right up the road in Columbus, was also a social gospel leader. His church, a United Church of Christ congregation, is still thriving in downtown Columbus.

Why are Americans so frightened by the possibility of socialism? No socialist can get elected president. Eugene Debs, our most famous socialist, ran for president 5 times. The highest percentage of votes he ever received: 5.99%. Bernie Sanders, the independent Vermont (isn't that an oxymoron?) senator is a socialist and he's running for president. Isn't that just like God? A secular Jew, running for a secular office, preaching the gospel and young adults responding with zeal, warms my heart.

Is Christianity socialist? Chronologically that is impossible. Christianity—founded 30 A.D.; Socialism—1848. Christianity came first and therefore can't be socialism but what's nineteen centuries to people who are paranoid about socialism? Some people refuse to let the facts get in the way of their beliefs. For true believers there are no hypotheses and this is the problem with the extreme left and extreme right. Blind faith wouldn't be blind if it could see the facts.

The two most famous people to think about money without reference to God are Adam Smith and Karl Marx. Smith saw us all as strangers. Karl Marx had an even worse view of human nature. He saw economics as a war. I find it ironic that the "war" metaphor is used by Marx in economics and by Christians in social issues. Marx saw us as all enemies. I don't care for Smith and Marx (or Smith and Wesson) and I have a word for both: "We are no longer strangers and aliens, but citizens with the saints and also members of the household of God. Biblical texts can be so unnerving when sacred cows are under attack.

Christianity is not socialism. We are children of God made for worship. Not strangers, but brothers and sisters in Christ. Not enemies but members of the body of Christ—one body, one God, one faith, one baptism. Paul tells us to invest in the economy of others. Paul tells us to develop a deep and lasting spirit of generosity that permeates all our relationships so that we are not bitter, angry, mistrustful, and cynical all the time about everything. Complete purity, complete sanctification, perfect holiness eludes everyone, but a generous spirit is available to everyone. The root word of economics is *oikonomia*—it means household management. Economics means putting your house in order. You are never going to be perfect and you certainly can't make everyone else be as holy as you would like, but you can have a generous spirit. Remember Barnabas from the book of Acts? He was generous with his money, with his support, with his encouragement. He was generous with people who failed and people who were different. And do you know the final word on Barnabas in the Bible? "He was a good man, full of the Holy Spirit." It doesn't get any better than that. Do you possess a generous spirit? Jesus is also our model here. Are you surprised that the cross is conceived in economic terms? "For you know the generous act of our Lord Jesus Christ, that though he was rich, yet for your sakes he became poor, so that by his poverty you might become rich." So we pray: "Forgive us our debts as we forgive our debtors." Forgiveness is an act of great generosity. "Forgive seventy-seven times." A generous spirit is the mother of forgiveness. With a generous spirit we can forgive seventy-seven times like Jesus insists. And wherever generosity lives, hospitality moves in with her.

I'm asking you to invest in the economy of Manna by producing generosity in large vats like fine wine spread it all over the place.[5] The Holy Spirit is here and she is whispering in our ears: "At my command, unleash generosity."

---

5. Isaiah 55:1–2, *NRSV*.

Response
Excel in Generosity

Emily Hunter McGowin

"Excel in Generosity" is an uncomfortable, stepping-on-toes kind of sermon. Where I come from in the land of Texas Baptists, they would call this a meddlin' sermon: "Brother Rod's meddlin' this morning!" And that is as it should be. I am not sure a preacher can address the topic of money faithfully in the American context without making most of the congregation fidget and squirm in the pews. And why is that? Because, as Kennedy says, "You cannot love God and money but, Jesus or no Jesus, we love both."

This sermon especially excels at diagnosing the mammon-loving sickness that plagues American Christians. We are the wealthiest country in the world and yet, for most of us, what we have is never enough. We don't want to be millionaires—just a little bit more than what we have right now. Even in church, Kennedy says, we are thinking about our portfolios and anxious about our debts. American Christians know in a theoretical way that "resurrection changes the way we think about economics," but putting that into practice is very difficult.

Of course, as Kennedy explains, we have the example of the early church, but even that is puzzling for American Christians. We read that they shared their goods, had everything in common, and sold property to give gifts to the poor and our first thought is, "That's socialism!" rather than "That's the church!" Kennedy is right to critique this peculiarly American fear of socialism. This is a vital point for a sermon of this sort because so many Christians have been inculcated to reject in a kneejerk way anything that infringes on private property and individual liberty. Kennedy defuses that reaction by distinguishing clearly between socialism as a secular economic model and the church-rooted practice of Christian generosity. Put simply, Christianity can't be socialism because the Christian economy is based on the resurrection. As Kennedy says, "We are children of God made for worship. Not strangers, but brothers and sisters in Christ. Not enemies but members of the body of Christ—one body, one God, one faith, one baptism." And it is out of this new identity that we can give ourselves over to "a deep and lasting spirit of generosity." In an age where left-leaning Christians can too easily equate the church's "economy of manna" with a particular economic policy, Kennedy preaches the uniqueness of the Christian's resurrection-based generosity. Even if we sympathize with Bernie Sanders' democratic socialism, Kennedy won't let us mistake that economic model for the gospel of Jesus Christ.

One of my favorite parts of "Excel in Generosity" is the beautiful contrasting language: "economy of mammon" versus the "economy of manna." Yet, I wanted Kennedy to say more about the economy of manna that Jesus models and calls us to. Perhaps it would have been helpful to hear more about this economy of manna from the story of God's people. My mind goes immediately to Hagar's flight into the Desert of Beersheba, or Israel's wilderness wanderings, or Elijah sulking in the caves of Mt. Horeb. All of these stories testify to the provision of God. Because "this is our Father's world," we need not covet, hoard, and fret about our daily bread. The economy of mammon is driven by scarcity and anxiety while the economy of manna is driven by faith, hope, and love.

In addition to reaching back to the larger story of God's people, I would have liked to hear more of a vision for what the "economy of manna" looks like. This is definitely the part of the sermon where I felt the most intrigued and challenged. There are many ways that I do not live in God's safe world of abundance and provision—and it is for this reason that I am not more generous. Instead, I hoard and hide, even if only in my heart. In recognition of my own need, I would have liked to know more about what Christian generosity looks like "on the ground" and why we can, in fact, give ourselves to this way of life. Kennedy skillfully tells us why the economy of mammon isn't Christian and why the economy of manna isn't socialism. But, then, what does the "alternative economy based on generosity" really look like? And why should we embrace this alternative economy?

Just as American Christians need to be convinced that sharing our goods isn't socialism, we also need to be convinced that the excellent generosity to which Jesus calls us is worth our commitment. Indeed, a life led by a "generous spirit" is an abundant life where we become more and more fully human.

At the end of Kennedy's sermon, the question I was left with was, "How do we do this?" How do we cultivate a spirit of generosity? How do we become the kinds of people who live within the economy of manna rather than mammon? I am convinced this is not the sort of transformation that can be accomplished by direct effort. Rather, the Holy Spirit cooperates with our habits and practices to change us slowly—very, very slowly. Kennedy is right to show us that forgiveness and hospitality emerge from a generous spirit, but I think more direction is needed on how to pursue that generous spirit. "Economics means putting your house in order," so how might a Christian go about doing this?

As it pertains to matters of tone and style, I think Kennedy strikes just the right note. His approach in "Excel in Generosity" is prophetic without bullying and persuasive without manipulating. Also, he includes just enough humor to provide some existential breaks within an uncomfortable topic. As I said above, this is a meddlin' sermon. But even meddlin' sermons can be received well when preached with warmth and humor. This sermon demonstrates that the preacher is very much on the side of his congregation (he includes himself among those for whom generosity is a challenge) and that can make all the difference in the congregation's response. Kennedy sorts through our mental furniture as it pertains to money and points out the problems with some of our most beloved pieces. And, rather than become annoyed at this intrusion, I finished the sermon interested to talk more about the implications.

Of course, no sermon can say everything—nor should it. The criticisms offered above naturally come from my own preferences and predilections as a preacher. Certainly, they do not take away from the real value in this message. I was, as scripture says, spurred on toward love and good deeds (Heb. 10:24). And that, I think, is very much the point.

Response
Excel in Generosity

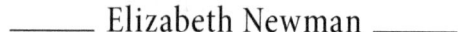 Elizabeth Newman

KENNEDY'S FINE SERMON, "EXCEL in Generosity," nicely exemplifies the conviction that we can only live in the world we can see. We easily assume economics is about the stock market, banking, investments, savings and all the hording and anxiety that surrounds these financial activities. But Kennedy reminds us just how myopic this account of economics really is. Not only does it easily divide families and discourage our youth, it also cripples our capacity to see ourselves as mutual participants in a Divine generosity. It blinds us to the truly good news that our economy, made possible by the death and resurrection of Christ, is one of *manna* rather than *mammon*. Kennedy offers that this economy differs as much from Jock loc.e's vision—where economy is interpreted through the lens of private property and individual accumulation—as it does from Karl Marx, whose economics is sustained by an inherent violence. If money is always embedded in our way of seeing ourselves and the world, then both of these accounts need corrective lens. Both hoarding and enmity run counter to the Biblical alternative based on generosity: "The one who had much did not have too much, and the one who had little did not have too little" (1 Cor 8:15). Kennedy appeals specifically to the generosity of Barnabas, pointing to the conviction that to participate in the life of the Holy Spirit is to take part in an economy of manna.

In addition to this lucid description of two vastly different economies, Kennedy insightfully points out that in the Scripture passage for his sermon, the cross itself is an economic act: "though he was *rich*, yet for your sakes he became *poor*, so that by his *poverty* you might become *rich*" (1 Cor 8:9, my emphasis). Kennedy thus alerts his listeners that the economy here envisaged flows from the heart of the Gospel. These passages are not so much economic rules as they are about seeing ourselves as part of the economic story of God with his people.[1]

Given the profundity of Kennedy's message, his sermonic refrain—"Don't pull that Bible stuff on us preacher"—fails in my view to capitalize on the richness of his vision. Might he have found a better refrain, one that focuses on this surprising economy of abundance? That money *has* a moral purpose, that the cross *is* an economy, that our economy is *not* about scarcity: any of these ideas sound strange to modern ears and would bear repeating.

Kennedy rightly engages some of the potential pushback for challenging our dominant culture's economic assumptions. One of these is the worry about socialism and I found his response only partially persuasive. He observes that Christianity was here before socialism and wonders why Americans are so frightened by the possibility of socialism. This "wonder" along with his reference to Bernie Sanders and his comments that "Democrats should be ashamed that they can't find more people to run for president" distract in that he seems to be no longer reframing how Christians think about economics, but accepting the terms of the American political debate. Since economics and politics are inextricably related, any renewal of one will call for a renewal of the other.[2] Can Kennedy state more fully

---

1. As Dietrich Bonhoeffer so powerfully emphasizes in *Life Together* (NY: HarperOne, 2009), listening to Scripture is not first of all about "applying" the Bible to our situation, but learning to see ourselves and our situations as part of the history of God with a people. Thus Bonhoeffer speaks of believers being "torn out of our own existence and set down in the midst of the holy history of God on earth," 53.

2. This point also applies to Walter Rauschenbusch, who Kennedy sympathetically cites. While Rauschenbusch rightly sought to expand American's understanding of the gospel to emphasize more fully its social reality, his politics remained deeply embedded in liberal democratic assumptions. As Stanley Hauerwas notes about Rauschenbusch, the church becomes " increasingly irrelevant for the project of changing America." Hauerwas notes that ethicists today continue to yearn, like Rauschenbusch, to "have public impact. Only now they no longer speak of 'Christianizing the social order' but of providing ethical analysis of 'policy options'" in Stanley Hauerwas, "Walter Rauschenbusch and the Saving of America," *A Better Hope, Resources for a Church Confronting Capitalism, Democracy, and Postmodernity* (Grand Rapids, MI: Brazos, 2000), 107.

why the economics of generosity does not fit on the democratic/republican political grid?

Kennedy's sermon can be helpfully related to Wendell Berry's wonderful essay, "Two Economies."[3] Berry observes that while our global, capitalistic economy sees itself as the *only* true economy, there is in fact another economy; Berry calls it the "Great Economy." This Great Economy, among other things, enables us to see ourselves as part of a larger whole. This Economy (which Berry identifies with the Kingdom of God) is not to be managed or controlled but recognized and received. Thus, says Berry, "Competitiveness cannot be the ruling principle, for the Great Economy is not a 'side' that we can join nor are there such 'sides' within it. Thus, it is not the 'sum of its parts' but a *membership* of parts inextricably joined to each other, indebted to each other, receiving significance and worth from each other and from the whole." The Great Economy excels in generosity.

Kennedy's sermon can likewise be favorably interpreted in relation to Pope Benedict's XVI encyclical *Caritas in Veritate*. Benedict describes a political economy sustained by a theological vision that is irreducibly relational: "all is ordered by the divine 'economy of charity' to the highest Good in God."[4] This economy of love, like Kennedy's economy of generosity, draws us to the truth of who we really are.

Kennedy's challenging sermon points us in a gospel direction: economics is ultimately not a sphere but a way of living. To unleash generosity is to participate, through the Spirit, is God's economy for all creation.

---

3. Wendell Berry, *Home Economics* (San Francisco: North Point, 1987), 72.

4. Adrian Pabst is describing the encyclical in "The Paradoxical Relation of the Good," in Adrian Pabst, editor *The Crisis of Global Capitalism, Pope Benedict XVI's Social Encyclical and the Future of Political Economy* (Cambridge: James Clarke & Co, 2011), 179.

4

A Scary Resurrection
Mark 16:1–8

IN THE MOVIE, *IMITATION Game*, we meet the genius mathematician Alan Turing. The year is 1951 and the man who helped break the Nazi Enigma code says to a police detective:

> Are you paying attention? Good. If you are not listening carefully, you will miss things. Important things. I will not pause, I will not repeat myself, and you will not interrupt me. You think that because you're sitting where you are, and I am sitting where I am, that you are in control of what is about to happen. You're mistaken. I am in control, because I know things that you do not know. What I need from you now is a commitment. You will listen closely, and you will not judge me until I am finished. If you cannot commit to this, then please leave the room. But if you choose to stay, remember you chose to be here. What happens from this moment forward is not my responsibility. It's yours. Pay attention.

Oh my, I have always wanted to say something like that to my congregation. Well, I just did that didn't I? I believe we can live full and flourishing lives and it has everything to do with Easter.

What we expect today is the happy ending! So welcome to Happy Ending Sunday! Truth be told, we like happy endings. We are a people of happy endings. We assume happy endings because our cultural religious canon—television and movies us happy endings. American movies have more messiahs than we can count!

Our critics claim that Christians are a bunch of naïve escapists, but a happy ending is not always escapist. But you can't have a happy ending just by expecting it or imagining it. We are not given a happy ending just for showing up. The struggle, the agony, the blood, sweat, and tears precede the happy ending. Otherwise, it is an illusion. Fear complicates happy endings. David Brooks has an essay called "On Conquering Fear."[1] What a sermon. Preaching was already too hard and now David Brooks, not a preacher, out preaches all of us preachers. "Everybody is afraid sometimes," he begins. "The fear makes people apathetic, torpid, and skeptical." Fear makes it impossible for us to hear words of hope. Using the book of Exodus as text, Brooks shows how the Israelite women, led by Miriam, helped their men overcome fear with sexiness, storytelling, and song. This is troublesome for us because American Christians are scared to death of sex, suspicious of storytelling with its pregnant metaphors and promiscuous multiple meanings, and too timid to really sing. Even resurrection can fail to dampen our dark fears. Perhaps you wonder where I got such an idea. As they entered the tomb, they saw a young man, dressed in a white robe, sitting on the right side; and they were alarmed. ⁶But he said to them, "Do not be alarmed; you are looking for Jesus of Nazareth, who was crucified. He has been raised; he is not here. Look, there is the place they laid him."⁷ The young man dressed in a white robe, sitting on the right side represents the preacher of resurrection. The right side is where the pulpit chair was placed in the early church. After the sermon, afraid.⁸ Even resurrection struggles to squelch the fears that dominate us.

Brooks quotes Avivah Zornberg, *The Particulars of Rapture*: "It is this fear that makes hearing and speech impossible: a defensive rigidity that narrows the channels and closes the apertures."[2] Our ears are plugged with fear. My grandmother Carrie, a Baptist preacher's wife, often told us, "Get the rooster shit out of your ears." Language has lost its power among us; as O'Connor put it: "When you can assume that your audience holds the same beliefs you do, you can relax a little and use more normal ways of talking to it; when you have to assume that it does not, then you have to make your vision apparent by shock—to the hard of hearing you shout."[3]

There's no way around this truth: Resurrection, by definition, requires that somebody be dead. The reason we can't have Easter as all sunshine and

---

1. Brooks, "On Conquering Fear."
2. Ibid.
3. O'Connor, *Mystery and Manners*, loc. 309–10.

fun is that we are participants in a wrong that was so wrong that we cannot make it right. The perfect man, who lived a life of perfect goodness—this man Jesus we raised up on a Roman cross of capital punishment. I am really glad that you are here today but its costs something to have the privilege of coming to Easter church.

How odd to end a book of good news with the word "afraid." The early church didn't like it either. Rather soon after Mark's gospel made the rounds of the churches and someone had already come up with a different ending. It is called the "short ending". Then someone else added the longer ending of Mark. It is this longer ending that makes impossible claims for the power Christians will possess: cast out demons, pick up snakes, and drink poison without dying. The longer ending reads more like Harry Potter, The Lord of the Rings, or any of Grimm's tales. Some people will believe anything to avoid facing the reality of fear. And so we imagine happy endings.

How odd that we expect happy endings and our movie world serves them to us as cheap escape, but the reality is that "living happily ever after" may be on life support. A Hi and Lois cartoon shows Dad reading a story to the children: "And they all lived reasonably content for the time being." The daughter asks, "What happed to 'Happily ever after'?" Then the son says, "At least they're not permanently miserable."

Look, resurrection was just as hard for the women to believe as it is for us. There's no shortage of Christian beliefs about the nature of resurrection. I am not concerned whether your resurrection belief comes from Billy Graham or Marcus Borg. For me what now matters is whether or not we are resurrected people filled with the promised power and joy of our "raised from the dead" Lord. It is a mistake to say the women didn't believe the resurrection. They believed but they were still scared. Scared belief is not a bad belief. I once did a seminar for the Sacred Heart Catholic Church in Fort Wayne, Indiana. When the education director mailed me the check she had spelled the name of her church as "Scared" Heart Catholic Church. This is the picture of our Christ-haunted lives: fearful believers. We worship with our fingers crossed. I will take that every Sunday. Pack up your fears and show up here and let us break bread together and share our lives and our stories. We live in a world where there are a number of different religious views on which intelligent, reasonable people can and do disagree.[4] We are

---

4. Charles Taylor, *A Secular Age*, 12. Taylor argues that the default setting is longer belief in God.

a people who look over our shoulders from time to time in a condition that is at times fearful. But it is precisely that loyal struggle that gives us hope.

I believe that we all want life to be fully satisfying and joyful. But often we know we are not there yet. Maybe we are not really living well but we are making a bold face: not fulfilled in primary relationship or vocation, not confident that we are making any real difference for the benefit of others. For whatever reasons maybe you are here with that dead feeling that refuses to give you peace in life. Resurrection can raise what is dead in your heart, dead in your job, dead in the dark nights of your soul, dead in your sense of boredom and feeling that this is all there is. There is no such thing as "this is all there is." How many live in a sort of middle earth where they have managed to stay busy enough and wealthy enough and absorbed in enough and shopping at the mall to escape the forms of negation, exile, emptiness, and guilt that haunts the edges of the human mind?

Here's the deal: Into our fear-drenched, white-knuckled world, God has poured resurrection power. The resurrection movies established forever the kingdom of Jesus Christ on earth. This is how it is going to be from now on: the poor, the mourners, the peacemakers, and those who hunger and thirst for righteousness shall be filled. An empty grave has no value to an empty stomach. An empty grave doesn't help an empty pocketbook. Jake Dorn recently reminded me that for too many preachers there is no word about the social implications of the gospel. In other words, the gospel is social or it isn't really good news. And that led to this sentence in my sermon: Resurrection means social justice or it isn't really good news.

One of our major fears, for example, is economic. The American litany is "Don't kill the goose that lays the golden eggs." We are told to fear those who are out to kill the goose that lays the golden eggs. I confess to some dark thoughts about the Canadian geese that are too lazy to fly south and insist on peppering our city with goose dung, but they lay no golden eggs. Isn't it strange that a people who think we no longer have a problem with idolatry worship a female goose that lays golden eggs? Long ago, the children of Israel worshiped a golden calf and we worship a golden goose. Is that moral progress? In the movie, *The Hobbit: Battle of the Five Armies*, the king of the dwarves, Thorin Oakenshield, is stricken with dragon sickness. What is dragon sickness? It is the growing desire and obsession with having more gold and the inability to part with even a single piece of gold. It's what happens when capitalism jumps the track and loses its ethical bearings. I am not debunking happy endings, but I am asking you not to put your trust in imagined happy endings. Easter is the ultimate happy ending but we have to participate in it. God has to "easter" in us the power of resurrection.

Resurrection belief, like grief, comes in stages. There's no other way to be resurrected but by passing through the cemetery in the dead of night. Being afraid is the first stage in believing the resurrection. It is followed by a sense of "this can't possibly be true" and then there is a rush of doubt and skepticism and a resistance to the reality and then there is acceptance and that is followed by joy. And this joy is followed by proclamation of the good news.

I want you to have as many happy endings as possible, but the one real happy ending is that Jesus has been raised from the dead. May all that is less than you have hoped be resurrected in you this grand day by the power that raised Jesus from the dead!

Response
A Scary Resurrection

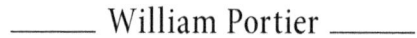 William Portier

As one whose church has not called him to proclaim the gospel to a congregation every Sunday, and, as one who has heard Dr. Kennedy preach, I approach the task of writing a "critique" of his Easter sermon with trepidation. Kennedy's text is the first eight verses of Mark's last chapter, his "original ending," as some have it. It ends starkly: "They said nothing to anyone, for they were afraid" (Mk 16.8). Fear silences us and keeps us from fully feeling the "resurrection power" God pours into "our fearful world." Kennedy wants us "to dampen our dark fears" so we can really hear the proclamation of Jesus's resurrection on Easter.

Throughout his gospel, Mark plays with fear and faith. Jesus himself juxtaposes them when he calms the storm in 4:40. He has been asleep in the disciples' boat, an ancient image for the church. "Why are you terrified?" he asks his fearful followers, "Do you not yet have faith?" The storm-tossed boat returns in Mk 6. Jesus walking on the water terrifies the disciples. They don't realize it was he coming toward them (6:50).

As in this last example, God's powerful acts cause fear. Earlier in the gospel, the cure of the Gerasene demoniac seizes the people with fear (5:15). After Jesus heals her, the woman suffering from a hemorrhage approaches him trembling with fear (5:33). To Jairus, the synagogue official whose daughter had just been reported dead, Jesus says simply, "Do not be afraid; just have faith" (5:36).

"Lord, I believe, help Thou my unbelief," (9:24), the prayer of another father pleading for an afflicted child, suggests that fear and faith are not simply juxtaposed. Neither are they incompatible nor mutually exclusive. Rather, as Kennedy makes clear, they are mixed together in varying proportions. The people who are afraid in Mark's gospel have approached Jesus. They want to believe. "They were on the way, going up to Jerusalem, and Jesus went ahead of them. They were amazed, and those who followed were afraid" (10:32). As in the Statler Brothers' old song, "Would You Recognize Jesus?" they have trouble making sense of the scheme of reckoning upon which God bases his mighty acts. We expect to see Jesus driving a chariot of the Lord, but he's more likely to arrive in a '49 Ford.

So, when we read in 16:8 that, upon hearing the first Easter proclamation, the loyal disciples, who had gone to anoint Jesus, fled in fear, we are shocked. As Kennedy emphasizes, however, believing in the deferred happy ending promised by Easter is hard. The women at the tomb "believed, but they were still scared." They were at faith's first stage. The Greek verb Mark most often uses for being afraid contains the root of our English word *phobia*. We have a phobia for God's mighty acts. They unsettle our expectations and our normal places in the world.

Instead of being surprised at this verse, we need to ask two questions: What are we afraid of? And who are *we*? Mark's disciples get really scared when Jesus starts talking about his own suffering and its connection to his messianic office (9:32). The chief priests and the scribes feared Jesus because of his effects on the crowds, and, by implication, their position (11:18; 12:12). Both groups worry about what will happen to their place in the scheme of things.

Kennedy speaks of "Christ-haunted" souls, including himself, who "worship with our fingers crossed." In the "loyal struggle" of "fearful believers" such as those we find in Mark, Kennedy speaks of resurrection raising "what is dead in your heart . . . dead in your sense of boredom and feeling that this is all there is." As a relatively well-off white Christian, I recognize what Kennedy evokes here. When I look up at the vastness of the night sky, I hope I'm looking at God's grandeur proclaimed. The thought of an unimaginably vast twinkling abyss haunts me just the same. But these are relatively comfortable, nearly domesticated fears.

Kennedy needs to remind people like me of other kinds of fears which might put meat on the bones of his gesture in the direction of social justice. He mentions our economic fears but then he loses me with the "female goose that lays golden eggs." Is this the free market? Why not say so? If not, what am I missing? Aren't there deeper fears? In a racially divided city such as Dayton, the kinds of fears that Ta-nehisi Coates relates to his son in *Between the World and Me* are alien to me as a white man. Facing them jeopardizes my position in the scheme of things, much as Jesus threatened the disciples with talk of his suffering, or the chief priests and the scribes by inspiring the crowds. Though related to them, these fears go deeper than economics, touching our familiar place in the world, threatening to overturn it in the interests of those who suffer unjustly.

First among the women who went to the tomb early on Easter morning is Mary Magdalen. Immediately following the original ending, she is identified as one "out of whom Jesus had driven seven demons" (16:9). In Mark, Jesus casting out demons was one of the things that made people afraid. Sure enough, when Mary proclaims the resurrection after Jesus appears to her, his companions close their ears and do not believe. To which Mary or prophetic Miriam proclaiming God's mighty acts are we closing our ears? What mighty acts is God now doing in our midst? How must we change our scheme of reckoning in order to recognize Jesus risen when he comes toward us?

5

Guess Who's Coming to Dinner
Mark 2:1–17; 14:3–10, 22–25

MEALS MATTER A LOT in our faith. Last Sunday I declared that radical egalitarianism is the good news of Jesus. Today I am going to add open commensality. It's a term from anthropology. Commensality—from *mensa*, the Latin word for "table." It means the rules of tabling and eating as miniature models for the rules of human relations. It means table fellowship as a map of economic discrimination, social hierarchy, and political differentiation. This is the image I will attempt to burn into our consciousness: The table in our homes is a miniature picture of our real values, beliefs, and relationships.

Start with Jesus will share a meal with anyone: social, moral, and political rejects. Mark, Q, and Luke's own special material show Jesus sharing meals with tax collectors and sinners. These are the people who, in high school, have to sit alone in the school cafeteria and are never allowed at the popular table, the cheerleader table, or the football players table. We should have learned from Jesus that we can't build up our righteousness by putting down the alleged unrighteous in our midst. We can tell that this was a major part of Jesus' life because his opponents berated him as a glutton, a drunkard, and a friend of tax collectors and sinners. He makes, in other words, no appropriate distinctions and discriminations like normal good people. This false name-calling is right there with the ones that claimed Jesus had no authority, that he was crazy, possessed by demons, and that he could not forgive sins. It's hard to know if the moralists thought his meal habits or being possessed of Satan was a higher criticism.

Recall the Pharisee's shock when Jesus didn't wash before eating. I once told my mother that Jesus didn't wash his hands before meals, and this daughter of a preacher man smiled and said, "Our Lord, unlike you, was without sin. Now wash your hands and your sins which are as scarlet shall be as white as snow." My mother's biblical knowledge was not a thing to be messed with by anyone.

Anthropologists tell us, "To know what, where, how, when, and with whom people eat is to know the character of their society."[1] Jesus is the embodiment of an absolute equality of people. "Food exchanges are basic to human interaction."[2] As goes the table, so goes the culture. This is why the oft-repeated argument, "We are not racists" rings false. In our homes, around our table, we are as segregated as the 1950's. There might as well be a sign on the dining room door, "Whites Only." At best, we are recovering racists.

Remember the movie "*Guess Who's Coming to Dinner*" starring Spencer Tracy, Katharine Hepburn, and Sidney Poitier? The film deals with a liberal family's discomfort at Joanna, their daughter's interracial marriage. They taught Joanna that all the races were equal. And they believed it until a man of another race was sitting at their table intending to marry their daughter. The plot of the movie unfolds around a meal and you can feel centuries of prejudice at play.

Guess who's coming to dinner? In the case of Jesus vs. the entire world of culture, religion, economics, and politics, there's no question: The poor are coming to dinner. The lepers are coming to dinner. The tax collectors (traitors to God and country) are coming to dinner. The Pharisees are coming to dinner.

In the truncated canon of many American liberal Christians, the meal stories of the gospels are in the top 10 beloved texts. Nothing is more thrilling to the liberal impulse in Christianity than Jesus consorting with sinners. New Testament scholar E. P. Sanders in *The Historical Figure of Jesus* says that Jesus never requires tax collectors and sinners to repent. All they had to do was accept him. Dominic Crossan disagrees with Sanders. "It is almost like praising a serial killer for paying his traffic fines."

---

1. Crossan, *Jesus A Radical Biography*, loc. 1396.
2. Ibid.

Today these Christians are the progressive party. They say, "The progressive, open-minded people are in and the judgmental bigots are out—and of course—we are the open-minded ones." There's an enormous amount of self-righteousness about self-righteousness. We think we are so much better than people who think they are better than other people. It is hard to resist the presumption that to be open-minded is to be good. To be judgmental is not good. Call it a category mistake. It's like a religious game of Jeopardy. "Alex, I'll take Open Mindedness for $1,000." But Jesus does not use these categories to separate the good from the bad.

Here we are looking down on people looking down on others and we have forgotten that God is looking down on us all. We think the good news is about the open-minded and the judgmental, but it's about the humble and the proud. As Will Campbell once said of himself, "I discovered that I was more prejudiced against the Rednecks than the Rednecks were prejudiced against blacks." Once you take what you consider the high moral ground, it is hard not to feel superior. The good news says the humble are in and the proud are out. The good news says that people who know they are not better, not more open-minded, not more moral than others, are in, and the people who think they are in the right and on the right side are most in danger. And in the middle are the ones who proudly say, "I just want everyone to be nice and get along with one another." They are so proud to be above the fray, but they are out as well.

Jesus is eating with tax collectors not endorsing the thievery of tax collectors. He is eating with sinners not approving the sinfulness of sinners. Jesus is eating with Pharisees not signing off on a religion of rules and regulations. Being invited to the table is not the same as bearing your cross. Jesus went home with Zacchaeus and had a meal with him. After sitting at table with Jesus, Zacchaeus repented of his economic crimes against the poor. Jesus eating with sinners makes no sense if he is not calling them to a life of holiness. Jesus came to Matthew's house for a meal, and this new disciple of Matthew had invited all his friends to meet Jesus at the table—and all his friends were tax collectors.

One day Jesus went to dinner at the home of a Pharisee named Simon. During the meal there was a party crasher. Luke calls her "a woman in the city, a sinner." She comes to the table with an alabaster jar of ointment. She kissed Jesus' feet and anointed them. A deeply offended Simon: "How did this woman get past security?" He accuses Jesus of being a false prophet because Jesus doesn't know this woman is a sinner. In Simon's nasty world of good vs. bad, of limited categories, a true prophet would not allow a sinner to touch him. Simon thinks that knowledge consists of knowing who the bad people are. Simon stands for those who think that only the good people are in God's kingdom and the bad people are out—and Simon and the Pharisees say, "And of course we are the good ones." It is hard to resist the presumption that to have strong moral scruples, to oppose what you think is immoral, is good. To have "family values" is good. To be open-minded is bad. But Jesus doesn't seem to use these descriptions to separate the good from the bad. To be either, from the perspective of Jesus, is a problem. It's like a religious game of Jeopardy: "Alex, I'll take moral scruples for $1,000."

But of all things, Jesus says, "Simon, do you see this woman? I entered your house; you gave me no water for my feet, but she has bathed my feet with her tears and dried them with her hair. You gave me no kiss, but from the time I came in she has not stopped kissing my feet. You did not anoint my head with oil, but she has anointed my feet with ointment." Simon violated all the rules of hospitality. "Therefore, I tell you, her sins, which were many, have been forgiven; hence she has shown great love." And he said to the woman, "Your faith has saved you; go in peace." The categories of Jesus: repentance, forgiveness, love, and faith.

Now, let's look at this same story through a different set of eyes. In Mark's story emphasis is on the woman of the street: "Truly I tell you, wherever the good news is proclaimed in the whole world, what she has done will be told in remembrance of her." Why is this unnamed woman so important? Why does she get this amazing praise from Jesus? Why isn't she more important in the early church than she is? The male disciples of Jesus were told three times by Jesus that he would die and rise again. Remember that Mark has a more critical view of the disciples than Matthew or Luke. "The disciples have never, as Mark sees it, understood or accepted Jesus' impending crucifixion. But now, in the home of Simon the Leper, for the first time somebody believes that Jesus is going to die and that unless his body is anointed now, it never will be".[3] Crossan then makes the remarkable suggestion that this story may be "Mark" herself obliquely and indirectly signing her narrative. Ah, "Mark" a woman! "We cannot ever be sure whether Mark was a woman or a man. We can, however, be absolutely sure that the author of this gospel chose an unnamed woman for the supreme model of Christian faith—for the faith that was there before, despite, or even because of Jesus' death. Easter, for her, came early that year.

---

3. See Mark 8:31–33, 9:30–32, and 10:32–37. Crossan, *Jesus*, loc.3601.

GUESS WHO'S COMING TO DINNER

The disciples never understood or accepted Jesus' impending death. But this unnamed woman—of all people—believes that Jesus is going to die and that unless his body is anointed now, it never will be. "Easter for her, came early that year."[4] An unnamed woman, a woman from the street, embraces the good news; the "good guys" not yet.

That puts us at the table for the meal that matters the most: The Lord's Supper. When [Jesus] was at the table with them, he took bread, blessed and broke it, and gave it to them. Note the action: took, blessed, broke, and gave. These verbs indicate equal serving as the food is distributed to all. The host performs the role of servant. As amazing as this is, there's something more here. Remember the meal at the home of Mary and Martha. "There they gave a dinner for him. Martha served." Martha served because that was the rule: female hosting and serving. So at the Last Supper, "far from reclining and being served, Jesus himself, serves, like any housewife, the same meal to all, including himself."[5] By now, the religious elite, with their rule book for meals—thicker than an old Yellow Pages and just as obsolete, are like the lady looking at a new Buick, trying to grasp that it really is a Buick and saying, "Oh my!" Now radical egalitarianism and open commensality merge as good news!

And yet look at the church today. Some will not serve communion to the divorced and re-married. Some will not serve children or the unbaptized. Some will not serve any but their own members. "It is somewhat surprising that this image of Jesus sharing meals with marginal people seems to have had little influence in the early church." Even Jesus had to repeat his lessons.

So who is coming to dinner? The table was and is a miniature model for society. When anthropologists study our civilization two thousand years from now, perhaps they will be shocked by our meal habits, especially by our loss of the table. We once thought that the family that eats together stays together and yet today we so rarely sit down at the table for a meal. It is loss of the Sabbath principle that we no longer take time in our restless lives to spend an hour or two at the table as families. Here are two scenes from two popular television shows. *The Big Bang Theory* frequently shows Sheldon, Leonard, Penny, Howard, and Raj eating together in the den out of boxes of food from a local restaurant. In other words, there's no table. Contrast that to the closing scene of every episode of *Blue Bloods*. In the

4. Ibid., loc.3609.
5. Ibid, loc. 3396.

Reagan family, four generations sit together at the table and share Sunday dinner. There's a blessing and at the end of the blessing the sign of the cross. Which of these two scenes is more like you and your family?

Maybe as a Lenten discipline, you could agree to have at least one meal each week at the table with the entire family present, or to have a meal with a friend. After the postlude, I invite you to continue our worship by taking nourishment from the table. We are going to have an enacted Lord's Supper without ritual, without liturgy. The elements will be bread, donut holes, cake, cookies, coffee, and juice, but the meaning will be that all equally share in the Eucharistic meal.

Response
Guess Who's Coming to Dinner?

 David Wheeler-Reed

MICHEL FOUCAULT ONCE SAID: "I believe that somebody who writes has not got the right to demand to be understood as he had wished to be when he was writing; that is to say from the moment when he writes he is no longer the owner of what he says, except in a legal sense."[1] When I read the biblical stories discussed in this sermon, I didn't understand them in the same way as Kennedy understands them. Yes I'd like to believe that Jesus was a "radical egalitarian," but there's enough evidence in the New Testament to raise doubts. Besides the concept of egalitarianism didn't exist until the French Revolution, so it seems somewhat odd for us to talk about Jesus as the harbinger of equality, when humanity hadn't thought up the concept until centuries after his death.

The idea of a "radical egalitarian" Jesus is relatively new. Elisabeth Schüssler Fiorenza's watershed book, *In Memory of Her*, paved the way for numerous feminist constructions of Christian origins, which suggest that the earliest Jesus' movement was remembered primarily as a "discipleship of equals."[2] Problems remain, however, with this kind of construction of the "historical" Jesus and his first followers. The biggest problem is that these constructions are inherently anti-Judaic. As Kathleen Corley relates: "In spite of the hard work of certain Christian and Jewish feminist scholars

---

1. From "Michel Foucault and Zen," quoted in Carette, *Religion and Culture*, 32.
2. Fiorenza, *In Memory of Her*.

to try to correct the formulation that Jesus was a feminist within a negative Jewish environment, many Christian writers continue to use a narrative of primitive Christianity which posits a time of pristine origins followed by decay—a discourse that ultimately serves an anti-Judaic function."[3] Though Kennedy isn't anti-Judaic, I fear his sermon on Jesus' "radical egalitarianism" falls into the same trap that many white, male, liberal, American preachers fall into time and again.

Building on the words of Corley, the idea that the earliest Jesus' movement was "egalitarian" creates a narrative which contends that shortly after the time of the historical Jesus, a kind of "Fall" occurred in which Paul and other Christians reversed Jesus' teachings on equality, favoring instead, a patriarchal Christianity much like we see in the Pastoral Epistles and writings of the Apostolic Fathers. Elizabeth Castelli has labeled this narrative a "myth of Christian origins." As she points out, this myth serves an "apologetic" function in that it serves the foundational purposes of both modern Christian feminism and modern Christian liberalism.[4] In its extreme forms, this construction declares that the teachings of Jesus established something unique for the ancient world. In other words, Jesus was the first to fully accept women as persons, reversing not only Greco-Roman but Jewish notions, which defined women as mere chattels. Unfortunately, this kind of construction misreads women of the Second Temple era.[5]

Perhaps the biggest stumbling block to a Jesus who preaches "radical egalitarianism" is the fact that not once does he condemn slavery. Slavery was everywhere in the ancient world. Take, for example, a quote from Philostratus's *Life of Apollonius*:

> And as they fared on into Mesopotamia, the tax gatherers who presided over the Bridge led them to the registry and asked them what they were taking out of the country with them. And Apollonius replied: "I am taking with me temperance, justice, virtue, continence, valor, discipline." And in this way he strung together a number of feminine nouns or names. The other, already scenting his own prequisites, said, "You must then write down in the register these female slaves." And Apollonius answered, "Impossible, for they are not female slaves that I am taking with me, but ladies of quality."[6]

3. Corley, *Women and the Historical Jesus*, 8.
4. Castelli and Taussig, "Introduction: Drawing Large and Startling Figures," 3–20.
5. See, for example, Ross S. Kraemer, "Jewish Women and Christian Origins," 35–49.
6. Philostratus, *Life of Apollonius*, 1:20

Whether the women mentioned in this passage are slaves or prostitutes is beside the point. Passages like this one are ubiquitous in the Roman world, since slaves were everywhere. One-third of the population of the Roman empire was made up of slaves, so if Jesus had condemned this insidious institution, yes, he would've been quite radical. But the parables of Jesus tell quite a different story.

Before anyone can say Jesus preached "radical egalitarianism," Matthew 18:21–35 must be given its due. This parable, known as "The Parable of the Unforgiving Servant," is so well known, that I won't recount it here. What's important for us to recognize is that while Jesus compares the Kingdom of Heaven to a king who wishes to settle accounts with his slaves, he never once condemns the selling of human beings into slavery. On the contrary, he seems to take for granted the institution of slavery. And he even warns his followers that no one will get out of jail until they've paid their debt in full. Yes, the parable is ultimately about forgiveness, but this would've been a perfect place for Jesus to talk about the equality of servant and master if he believed in "radical egalitarianism."

Things get worse with a brief saying at Luke 12:47. Here Jesus condemns anyone who knows their master's will and doesn't do it. In what is surely one of the most shocking statements from Jesus' lips, he proclaims that the one who disobeys their master should be beaten. And at Matthew 24:51, he declares that masters have a right to kill their slaves if the slaves are disobedient. How is this a liberal, radical egalitarian Jesus preaching a gospel of tolerance and equality?

In his provocative book, *Sex and the Single Savior*, Dale Martin points out that "all interpretation is subjective and interested, that peoples interpretations of texts, even those about Jesus, are a product of who they are and where they live."[7] He continues by noting that we all come up with numerous images of Jesus—it's just what we do. I rely on Martin's wisdom here because I think he's right. And I think that what Kennedy has given us in his sermon is *one* among *many* interpretations of Jesus, but he fails to note that this is what he's doing. Is his construction of Jesus as a preacher of "radical egalitarianism" the historical Jesus? No. Is his reading wrong? No. What's wrong is that he fails to admit that he isn't *reconstructing* Jesus, but creating a *construction* of him based on his own geographical locale and life experiences.

---

7 Martin, *Sex and the Single Savior*, 101.

What puzzles me the most about Kennedy's sermon—and others like it—is why does he insist on Jesus being a champion of equal rights? Does it matter if he was? Does it matter if he wasn't? For Kennedy, it seems like it does matter. But why not admit that Jesus might've believed things that many of us no longer accept? Why not critique him and say that he was wrong?

Since I began this response with a quote from Foucault, I'll return to him once again. Speaking about the "role of the intellectual," he muses:

> The role of the intellectual is not to tell others what they have to do. By what right would he do so?. . . The work of an intellectual is not to shape others' political will; it is, through the analysis that he carries out in his field, to question over and over again what is postulated as self-evident, to disturb people's mental habits, the way they do and think things, to dissipate what is familiar and accepted, to reexamine rules and institutions and on the basis of this re-problematization (in which he carries out his specific task as an intellectual) to participate in the formation of a political will (in which he has his role as a citizen to play).

My goal throughout this response has been to "disturb people's mental habits" and to question what Kennedy thinks is "self-evident." I've no right to tell him what to do nor to shape him to my own way of thinking. Like I said above, I'd be quite elated if Jesus really was a preacher of "radical egalitarianism," but far too many questions remain for me to reach that conclusion. Ultimately, I think what Kennedy has presented us with is his own Jesus, which is a *construction*, but not a *reconstruction*, of the historical Jesus.

6

What Have We Done with the Good News?

Mark 1

WE DON'T KNOW MUCH of what happened to the followers of Jesus from 30 A.D. to around the 50's. Luke gives us information about Christianity moving from Jerusalem to Rome. There's nothing about Christianity in Galilee, precious little about the Twelve Apostles or the 70 witnesses or the 500 brothers and sisters ("most of whom are still alive") who saw Jesus after his resurrection. Borrowing a bit from Foucault I want to suggest that ordinary, nameless people are the actors in history, the gospel-producers. Glance through the gospel of Mark and meet these nameless people who spread the good news of Jesus before we had any written gospels.

Let the leper healed in Mark 1 speak for all the ordinary people. Mark says, "He went out and began to proclaim [his healing] freely, and to spread the word." So you think that you are ordinary, that you don't count, that you haven't ever made a difference? Look at these ordinary people. They kept the gospel alive until Mark could write it down. Listen you count! You are the spreaders of the good news!

Mark's gospel was written first. From the beginning, we see that the radical nature of the gospel made it difficult to swallow whole. The church has a complex and dangerous history of modifying the gospel to align with the culture.

Mark tells us that the good news is the kingdom of God has come! The new kingdom displaces the old kingdoms of nation, religion, and race. It challenges the hierarchies, distinctions, and discriminations of the culture. The kingdom of God brings a radical egalitarianism. "The equal sharing of spiritual and material gifts, of miracle and table, cannot be centered in one place because that very notion of place, of here over there, of this place over other places, symbolically destroys the radical egalitarianism it announces."[1] Every wall Jesus breaches, we try to rebuild. Every barrier Jesus knocks down, we try to put back. In the book of Acts, the egalitarianism is in full display. The church selects a replacement apostle for Judas and they do it by lot. A lottery for the 12th apostle. We understand lotteries don't we? How many of you dream of winning the mega-lottery? Would you have wanted to win the 12th apostle lottery? By the end of the 1st century, the lottery has been displaced with bishops, presbyters, deacons, and all kinds of hierarchical divisions. Now cardinals (a bunch of old men) elect the Pope (a man) and the world awaits the puff of white smoke. Imagine the 2016 presidential election decided by casting lots. Put 8 candidates from each party in a lottery machine, give it a spin, and pull out a name. And we have a president. Crazy talk, but it would save the Koch brothers a billion dollars and save us a year of mean, awful, painful, lying-through-the-teeth television advertising. The point is that the church struggles to maintain the radical egalitarianism of Jesus.

Let me try to demonstrate from a couple of scenes in Mark 1. When Jesus came to Capernaum, to the house of Peter, he healed Peter's mother-in-law and then everyone starting bringing the sick to Peter's house. This is not a disturbing miracle because it is in-house. We are good at in-house gospel stuff: Our family, our people, our place, our nation, and our church. Peter is the first to be called to follow Jesus, the first to suggest a different route. Peter was always trying to get Jesus to change course instead of following. "Get behind me Satan!" Peter grasped the notion that he could become Jesus' broker and help him gather the people and the kingdom would come to pass in Peter's house. Perhaps in some ways, the Roman Catholic Church has never let go of the idea of localizing the church in Peter's house. But Jesus refuses to stay put. "Let us go on to the next towns, so that I may preach there also; for that is why I came out."

Peter argues that it makes more sense to stay at Capernaum, and await the crowds. Peter and Jesus, not for the last time, have different visions of

---

1. Crossan, *Jesus: A Radical Biography*, loc. 1937.

mission. Jesus says, "Go;" Peter says "Stay." This is always the tension. Keep the kingdom in Jerusalem would be the cry by A.D. 40. Keep the kingdom for Jews only would be the cry by Acts 15. Keep the kingdom for Catholics only the cry of the Middle Ages. Keep America for Americans. Let me ask, "Is your Gospel, the one that guides your life, 'made in the USA?'" We prefer in-house gospels. The churches of American are being held hostage by alien politics—alien to the gospel of Jesus.

The message of the gospel confronted social oppression, cultural materialism, and imperial domination in the first and second centuries. The gospel does this work in every century and in every culture. And in every century the church undoes this work or at least tries. This is hard work but we have to keep asking: Are we following Jesus or making up a different gospel?

Mark connects the good news with the healing of a leper. Of all things, the radical move is that Jesus touches a leper. The word translated "leprosy" was a generic term for all skin diseases.[2] To touch a leper was a social mistake, a religious sin, a criminal act. Everyone knew that you didn't touch lepers. Once you touch a man condemned by social structures, you have a social gospel. Are you aware that it was Karl Marx that taught that Christianity conditions people to accept injustice by dreaming of heaven by and by? Hundreds of millions of people have been taught, by Marx and Communism, that Christianity is hostile to concern for social justice for the poor. Given the fact that Jesus' ministry focused on social and economic justice and that we was crucified by the political establishment with the aid of a corrupt religious establishment, a greater lie is hard to imagine. And you have the nerve to call me a socialist. Like touching a long row of standing straight-up dominoes, the touch of Jesus caused all kingdoms, kings, emperors, and empires to fall. The powers and the principalities heard the dominoes falling and they began the conspiracy right then and there that would nail Jesus to a cross.

The culture of Capernaum was built on shame, and the religious leaders had the power to dispense shame. The leper was not a social threat because of medical contagion, threatening infection, or epidemic, but because of symbolic contamination, threatening the security of society at large. Religious people can be shame-spreading experts. They can spread it all around and stack it to the ceiling.

Shame sticks to your insides like Velcro; it's shelf-life is decades-long. When I was fifteen, a woman ran a red light and hit my car on the driver's

---

2. Crossan, loc. 1541–43.

side. Her husband owned a local furniture store and he was the first person on the scene because his store was a block away from the accident. He took charge, told the police I was speeding and that was a lie. But what hurt were the words: "He's just a poor white trash kid from the country. Never will amount to anything. It was his fault." My daddy got there and he took care of business in his quiet, humble way. Then he turned to me and saw the tears in my eyes and he grabbed me and hugged me. I didn't even need to tell him what happened; he knew. He hugged me fiercely and whispered, "Son, you are smarter than all of them put together. I love you." I still have residual resentment from being considered poor and ignorant, but my daddy's words trump those feelings every time. All the way from heaven, I can hear my daddy telling me he was proud of me. And here's a dirty little secret. One of the reasons I loved baseball so much is that it is the great equalizer. Being rich or living in town didn't do those boys one bit of good when I blew two fastballs past them on the outside corner and then when they were leaning over the plate for the next pitch, there came Suzy Q: a vicious dirt-seeking knuckle curve under the hands and the umpire's call of "Strike three!" My first cousin, Junior dug down in the dirt and nestled that pitch into his catcher's mitt and came up throwing the ball to the third baseman and saying "Atta boy." There's no equalizer like a sharp breaking curve in the dirt.

Why would Jesus risk the resentment of the entire culture? Mark tells us why: Moved with pity. He takes the shame of the leper. The good news is not just words but also actions. We too are to be a people of mercy. Spread as much mercy as possible. Put a sign outside our church: "Get your mercy here, America!"

Luke tells a story of Jesus healing 10 lepers. Luke portrays Jesus as an observant Jew. Luke puts Jesus back in the cultural box and there he keeps him very well. The lepers keep their distance. Jesus sees them but never comes close enough to touch. Jesus sends the lepers immediately to the Temple. They are healed on the way—no touching. In Mark Jesus touches a leper and destroys cultural boundaries; in Luke Jesus keeps his place in polite society. Jesus died for something more than how we do things around here, something more than the status quo, our cultural rules, customs, habits, and arrangements of power. Crossan says, "To remove that which is radically subversive, socially revolutionary, and politically dangerous from Jesus' actions is to leave his life meaningless and his death inexplicable." Which story do you prefer? Mark's destruction of cultural and religious rules or Luke's culture and religion aligned? We have invented family values in a gospel that teaches us that the family should be a secondary concern with our following Jesus first. We have invented a form of nationalism that demonizes other religions and other peoples. We have invented a righteousness that makes us superior to all the other nations of the world. We have invested patriotism with spiritual significance and pass it off as a Christian virtue as if that kind of delusion can justify the people we kill. Are we following the gospel or modifying its difficulty to suit our American tastes? Well, our modifying work has been so pervasive I think someone could write a book called "Christian False Gospels of America." Make a list of what Jesus condemned and see if we have turned those practices into false gospels: nationalism, wealth, and violence?

The gospel is the way of Jesus—not my way or your way. The gospel is a way of life—a path to be walked, a set of practices to be embodied in our daily actions. To follow the way of Jesus is an enacted metaphor. It is something we do each new day.

The invitation to follow Jesus is an invitation to take the Jesus way. Perhaps the first four disciples thought they would be home by dinner. It turned out to be far more and maybe that explains why the disciples always seemed to not get it. That is, of course, far different from Jesus' current bunch: We think we know the mind of Jesus about every subject

There's confusion here because Jesus seems to be going in all directions at the same time. When I went to Minneapolis for the first time, I was confused by the Interstate signs. I94 WSW completely befuddled me. Not only was I unable to talk "Minnestoan," "yah", but y'all I couldn't read the road signs. How do we know if we are actually following Jesus?

The good news begins with repentance. To repent means to change the mind. Repentance can only happen among people willing to examine their innermost thoughts, motivations, prejudices, and attitudes toward God and others. The "body of Christ" has a split personality. Some of Jesus' followers think we should share the wealth; other of Jesus' followers think that is nasty socialism. Some of Jesus' followers think we should welcome Mexican immigrants, others not so much. Some of Jesus' followers think we are destroying the environment; others that we are inhibiting the economy. Some of Jesus' followers think that the rich getting very, very, very richer while the poor get even poorer is sinful; others that the poor should get jobs and work. Some of Jesus' followers thinks FOX carries news; others NOT. Some of Jesus' followers think America is God's favorite; others bemoan the idolatry of nationalism. Jesus is not on everyone's side and he may not be on our side. We are facing division we do not know how to heal. Many may not want to have our alienation from one another healed. Hopeless divisions it seems. I am not sure what to do. I will leave that to you and your willingness to let the gospel read you.

There are plenty of Americans who see no need to confess our national sins. Jonah Goldberg made a recent theological assumption that deserves a moment long enough to consign it to Sheol. He claims Americans have the right to sit on our high horse and judge whomever we please. Jesus says, "If I be lifted up I will draw all people unto me." High horse or high cross?

In C. S. Lewis' *The Voyage of the Dawn Treader*, he tells the story of a boy named Eustace, and everybody hates him and he hates everybody. But he finds himself magically on a boat, the Dawn Treader. The boat pulls in to an island and Eustace finds a cave filled with treasure. "I'm rich," he cries. He plans to get even with everyone. He then falls asleep on the heap of gold and diamonds—which he doesn't know belongs to a dragon. Falling asleep with greedy dragonish thoughts, when he wakes up, he's become a dragon—big, terrible, ugly. One day the great lion Aslan shows up, leads him to a clear pool of water, and tells him to undress and jump in. He realizes that "undress" means to take off the dragon skin. He manages to peel off one layer but there are now multiple layers. In the end, Aslan says, "You're going to have to let me go deeper."

Eustace says: "I was afraid of his claws, I can tell you, but I was pretty desperate now . . . The very first tear he made was so deep that I thought it had gone right into my heart. And when he began pulling the skin off, it hurt worse than anything I've ever felt . . . Well, he peeled the beastly stuff right off, and there it was lying on the grass—thicker, darker, more knobbly-looking than I had imagined . . . Then he threw me into the water. It smarted like anything but only for a moment . . . Then I saw . . . I'd turned into a boy again."[3]

Maybe it is not that we have modified the gospel, maybe it is that our resistance to it has turned us into dragons, and after all these years we have layers and layers of thick gospel-resistant skin. We have to stop being afraid of the radical good news and let Jesus do his work of changing us into his followers. Will you be the radical dispenser of forgiveness, mercy, open sharing, and radical egalitarianism? If so the gospel is for you.

---

3. Keller, *Jesus the King*, 29.

Response
What Have We Done with the Good News?

 Philip E. Thompson

RODNEY KENNEDY AND I are Baptists. Each in our own way, we seek to remain faithful to the best in our Baptist heritage while shedding critical light on other aspects. Though Kennedy does not make explicit reference to Baptist history in this sermon, it is a deeply Baptist sermon. I will, however, offer a response grounded in Baptist history. Kennedy's and my shared heritage and commitments to that heritage put us on different sides of some of the questions his sermon raises. I offer here an invitation to reconsideration.

It would be impossible for me to address everything about this sermon. I will focus my critique on certain conceptual aspects alone. Subjects such as shame, repentance, and conversion, important as they are, must be left unattended, so too the structure of the sermon. My comments will have to do with what I take to be the two most important questions Kennedy is raising for us.

First is the role of those who he describes as nameless, ordinary folk who spread the gospel even prior to the writing of the canonical Gospels, and who have continued to do so throughout the church's history. Second, there is what Kennedy calls the modification of the gospel in order to align it more with cultural norms and mores. "Modification" is too tame a word. Kennedy leaves little doubt that it is more properly called a compromise or distortion.

Both of these are historically Baptist concerns. Baptists at their best have understood that the gospel is free and creates its own conditions of freedom. This dynamic includes the raising up of persons marginalized by official structures as proclaimers of this gospel freedom, and the naming of those official structures as idols seeking to usurp the freedom of the gospel. Among the abundant examples of this in Baptist history, we find Thomas Grantham cast the matter poetically mid-seventeenth century in *The Prisoner Against the Prelate*:

> But O the times, are they not perilous
> To publish Truth in? mind how quarrellous
> Is this poor Age against such, as would tear
> the hood of blind Devotion from their Ear
> And Eye, that so the Antient Gospel-pathes
> Might extirpate our fears, our jarrs, our wraths.
> But oh! Speak of this matter, and Sedition
> Is charg'd upon us, or a deep suspicion
> We must lye under; as, if to the Peace,
> Some danger by our freedom would increase. . . .[1]

The store of such declarations to this effect is large.

Kennedy does not develop this topic as much as he might because the related concern of the Gospel's distortion emerges more forcefully still. Here he sounds more like Baptists of the nineteenth century, after an important shift had occurred in Baptist thought. Earlier Baptists believed that the distorting compromise of the gospel lay with the usurpation of spiritual authority by the state through the state church. "(A)ll the power on Earth cannot make one Institute or Divine ceremony in Religion," asserted Grantham, "because (as we conceive) God's Authority is then usurped by Man, and Mens Fear towards him is then taught by the precepts of Men."[2] In the late eighteenth and early nineteenth centuries in the new United States, that charge was displaced to the church as an institution. There was suspicion of any authority external to the autonomous self.

To his credit, Kennedy does not say this. Yet it sounds implicitly in some of his claims, resulting in some assertions I found forced and unconvincing. Perhaps the greatest example of this is his setting of Luke and

---

1. Grantham, *The Prisoner Against the Prelate*, 3. Original spelling is retained in all quoted material.

2. Grantham, *Apology for the Baptized Believers*, 8, 10.

Mark against each other. While Kennedy is not making wholesale claims, it does seem an incongruous charge against the Third Gospel, which more explicitly expresses God's "option for the poor" than the others. Luke gives us the Song of Mary declaring the gospel's radical upending of hierarchies (1.52–53); Christ's beatitude upon the poor and the hungry, with corresponding woes pronounced upon the rich and satisfied (6.20–26); and in which Jesus notes as a sign of the Kingdom of God, "the blind receive their sight, the lame walk, the lepers are cleansed, the deaf hear, the dead are raised, the poor have good news brought to them. And blessed is anyone who takes no offence at me." (7.22–23) Culture and religion aligned?

Kennedy's concern for the ordinary and nameless proclaimers of the gospel is correct. Yet the fire of this egalitarianism needs the fireplace of the church with its structures. Are they liable to distort the gospel? Yes. Yet so is egalitarianism so radical it accepts no authority external to the self. So Grantham:

> [W]here the form of Godliness is neglected, Religion will in a little time either vanish, or become an unknown conceit, every man being at liberty to follow (what he supposes to be) the motions of the Spirit of God, in which there is so great a probability of being mistaken as in nothing more; for Man's ignorance being very great, and Satan very subtile, and the way of the Lord neglected, Men ly open to every fancy which pleaseth best. . . .[3]

Early Baptists' understanding of the "form of Godliness" was ecclesial through and through. Though they saw the state church as fatally compromised, and indeed saw all churches as potentially usurping the place of Christ, they believed that it was to the true church, with its creeds, sacraments, and duly ordained ministry, that "all persons that seek for eternal life, should gladly join themselves."[4] The radically free gospel becomes a formed and free people, whose life together is ordered to enable them to preserve this witness to radical freedom.

---

3. Thomas Grantham *Christianismus Primitivus, or The Ancient Christian Religion* Book II (London: n.p. 1678) p. 2.

4. "An Orthodox Creed, Or A Protestant Confession of Faith" (London, 1679), Article XXX in William L. Lumpkin and Bill J. Leonard, eds, *Baptist Confessions of Faith*, second rev. ed. (Valley Forge: Judson Press, 2011), p. 328.

7

Is there an unforgivable sin?
Mark 3:20–30

THE ONLY UNFORGIVABLE SIN is the refusal to ask for forgiveness. Jesus died for the sins of the world. A *Blue Blood* episode had a disturbing scene were a young woman confronted the man who had killed her parents and her seven-year-old brother. The killer told her that he had found God, and that when he realized what he had done he had tried to kill himself, and that he was now working to help other prisoners. The young woman was not buying it. She told him that he should try to kill himself again and this time he should succeed. She said, "I will never forgive you." It was a chilling moment and there's not a one of us who doesn't understand the young woman, but she is not Jesus. In our hearts we know that Jesus would forgive murderers. He was hung between two men of violence and he cried from the cross, "Father forgive them."

But here in our Mark text we are confronted with words about unforgivable sin. In fact, we get a word mob! Blasphemy! Beelzebub! Ruler of demons! Unforgivable sin! Satan! A strong man! I assume that you didn't lose any sleep this week worrying about whether or not you have blasphemed.

These verses are known in rhetoric as a contrapuntal.[1] They introduce an opposition, a different point of view. Jesus claims to be speaking with the

---

1. Contrapuntal is counterpoint. It is found extensively in the Baroque era (Bach, Handel). A fugue would be counterpoint, where you have polyphony, many voices. Bach wrote 48 Preludes and Fugues for the piano (harpsichord) and you will hear when the different voices enter into the music (Debbie Lindley).

IS THERE AN UNFORGIVABLE SIN?

authority of God. Mark says Jesus is the son of God. The scribes claim Jesus is Beelzebub, that he casts out demons by the power of Satan, and that he is a blasphemer. Back in chapter 2, Jesus forgives the sins of a paralytic and the scribes cry "Blasphemer." This is all about forgiveness and these scribes are not big on forgiveness.

"Your sins are forgiven!" The church knows this is the gospel. These words have been part of our liturgy from the beginning. "Almighty God have mercy on you, forgive you all your sins through our Lord Jesus Christ, strengthen you in all goodness, and by the power of the Holy Spirit keep you eternal life."[2] "May the almighty and merciful Lord grant us remission of all our sins, true repentance, amendment of life, and the grace and consolation of the Holy Spirit."[3] "In the name of Jesus Christ, you are forgiven!"[4]

Baptists are not quite convinced about the power to forgive sins because we say only God can forgive sins. So Baptist pastors don't usually pronounce forgiveness of sins. How odd this feels! Isn't it ironic that the scribes are the first to raise the issue that only God can forgive sins? I find it unsettling that we often act more like "scribes and Pharisees" than Christians. Ask yourself, "Am I more like Saul the Pharisee attempting to destroy his enemies with a scorched earth policy or am I more like St. Paul preaching the gospel to the world?" Well, we need to hear and know that our sins are forgiven and under the authority of the priesthood of believers we can say to one another—"Your sins are forgiven." Since so many preachers claim the authority to condemn, I claim the authority to forgive in the name of the one who is forgiveness. More than good advice, positive thinking, motivation, pep talks, and sweet Jesus stories, we need words of assurance, pardon, and forgiveness.

Blasphemer sounds like a word that has broken out of the prison that good people call profanity. You blasphemer! Most of us have been taught that it means to use God's name in vain. But it is much more than that. Here in Mark it means ascribing the work of Jesus to the devil. To blaspheme is to use the name of Jesus to validate causes that Jesus would oppose.

I once thought that repeated accusations about someone were an invention of our current excuse for politics. But it is an ancient failure of humanity. After all, the scribes kept accusing Jesus of blasphemy until they

---

2. *Book of Common Prayer*, 360.
3. *The United Methodist Book of Worship*, 475
4. Ibid, 35.

made it stick.[5] Robert McElvaine says there are no hypotheses for persons of faith, only facts.[6] If you repeat false charges often enough, the public will swallow them hook, line, and sinker. In the last week of Jesus' life he was put on trial for the crime of blasphemy. And they killed the blasphemer. Make the connection. For 3 years they repeated blasphemer, blasphemer. In the market, the temple, the streets, the coffee shops, the synagogue parking lots. Blasphemer turned into "Crucify him, crucify him." And they felt righteous and justified.

After any great truth is presented, there will always be a harsh reaction. There is no fury like a lie confronted with a new truth. The gospel's glaring white-hot light shines into the creepy shadows of our dead ways and scares us. We prefer what we think we know to any uncertainty.

We demonize what we oppose and we deny what we don't want to hear. The scribes demonize Jesus with a slogan. Jesus is a blasphemer. Slogans are short, slippery little devils. They fit on car bumpers and tweets. They easily go viral. As a child I was scared to death of the word blasphemy. I grew up listening to preachers go on until doom's day about the unforgivable sin. One preacher even said that you only had so many chances to say "YES" to Jesus and if you said "NO" too many times, you would have crossed the line and would be lost for eternity even if you lived another fifty years. I didn't really know what "blasphemy" was but I was both scared and excited by such a nasty-sounding word. I was drawn to all things religious at an early age. Lee Smith, writer of "Tongues of Fire," had a similar sort of experience. She says: "I would tell a friend that my grandmother had died and then I would go to my room and fling myself to the floor and pray without ceasing that my lie would not be found out, and that my grandmother would not really die. I made big deals with God—if He would make sure I got away with it this time, if Mama did not find out, I would sit with Lurice May at lunch on Monday (a dirty girl who kept her head wrapped up in a scarf and was rumored to have lice). I would give back the perfume and the ankle bracelet I had stolen from Ashely [my sister], and I would put two dollars of my saved-up babysitting money in the collection plate at church on Sunday. It was the best I could do." [God] did His part; I did mine. I grew in power every day." This is my story.[7]

---

5. Mark 2:7—"Why does this fellow speak in this way? It is blasphemy! Who can forgive sins but God alone?"

6. McElvaine, *The Great Depression: 1929–1941*, xix.

7. Smith, "Tongues of Fire," 17.

Blasphemy, it turns out, is a lot more serious than my boyhood misconceptions. Mark specifically tells us that blasphemy is attributing demonic power to the liberating and healing power of Jesus. Now, the scribes appear—the voice of religious authority—and they claim that Jesus is "possessed by Beelzebul." This obscure name never occurs in the Old Testament. In the New Testament it is found only here and in Q (Luke 11:15, 18–19; Matthew 10:25; 12:24, 27. Probably the name derives from the name of the Canaanite god meaning "Baal the Prince." Baalzebub ("Lord of the Flies") appears in 2 Kings 1:3, 6. Perhaps Mark adds "by the prince of demons" to explain to his Greek readers the strange phrase "he has Beelzebul." I take this Markan duplication to indicate that Jesus is being accused of working on the side of and being possessed by Satan. Since Mark's audience already knows of Jesus' victory over Satan in the wilderness, they know that this is a false and trumped up charge, but in that day, and in ours, accusations never have to be based on truth or reality or fact. They can be the wild imagination of anyone with a platform.

Jesus is accused of working for the devil. Jesus has come to destroy Satan not to make an alliance. Satan is the biblical word for all the forces that are aligned against God's purpose in this world. Evil has power but not enough to stop Jesus. Death has power; but it can't hold Jesus. The stronger one is Jesus.

Turns out that blasphemy is opposition to the gospel. And we need to look into our own hearts and dare to ask, "Is it us O Lord? Are we the ones who are trampling under our snow-streaked boots the good news of Jesus Christ? When we claim that our causes are the ways of the gospel, we may be guilty of blasphemy. Jesus' family tried to arrest him, take him by force and stop him from preaching the good news. Today that would be the churches. And in what ways are we trying to take Jesus by force and make him support our blasphemy? Sometimes Jesus is the square peg and our cause is the round hole and the two will not fit. As much as I am tempted to make the charge of blasphemy, and I speak humanly as a sinner, as much as I would like to give you a list of the 12 biggest blasphemers in our country, I am not sure how that might be done. If I started pointing fingers and saying, "You are a blasphemer and you are a blasphemer", my nose would start to grow. I am not sure how to draw up the sides and I am convinced it would be a mistake to engage in that kind of judgment.

So I have a different suggestion: I invite your attention to Isaiah 53 as a response to our tendency to blaspheme others. The gospel words are "us" and "our" and "all" and "y'all". Borrowing from one of my mentors, Carlyle Marney, Isaiah 53 is a report on a medical chart clipboard attached to the bottom of a hospital bed. Isaiah 53 is "lofty, devastating music which only strings and reeds can carry. The music for brass and tympani comes later." There is a cosmic backdrop—with Israel and the nations and Yahweh at the center. The drama keeps being replayed in every generation as only the actors and the names of the nations change.

We see the Sufferer and if honest, we cry, "My God, that's the same thing I've got!" It is our sickness the Sufferer has. This is known as identification, the religious miracle. We peer over the hospital bed and see our faces. It's not just the other side that is sick. It's not just those we despise who are on the verge of death. It is our sickness.

Identification is not easy. We have all forgotten the old truth of Donne: "If a clod be washed away by the sea, [the world] is the less, any man's death diminishes me." The words of our symptoms leap from the stage: our sicknesses, our pains, our chastisement, our transgressions, our iniquities. They tumble down the chart fastened to the foot of the bed like an avalanche of disaster—and the name on the chart is ours! It is our sickness!

But there is a new word, a gospel word: Redemption! Look at the other column of the chart, opposite the symptoms. On the treatment side are other verbal clues: he bore, he carried, was upon him, he was pierced, he was crushed. Look at the signature at the bottom. The physician is the Lord the Creator-Redeemer. We are forever under the treatment and care of our Holy Healer Lord. And by his stripes we are healed.

Do we get it now? All our demonizing and denying crucify our Lord again and again. It is the Lord who comforts, forgives, helps, and redeems. It is the Lord who promises to restore the land, to heal all the nations. Jesus is the stronger one who defeats all evil. He can be trusted and we can stop living in fear of one another. That is the good news for today!

Response
Is There an Unforgivable Sin?

 Derek C. Hatch _____

ROD KENNEDY OFFERS THIS homily centering on the hermeneutically-difficult question of blasphemy against the Holy Spirit. Much ink has been spilled and much sermonic effort has been given to figuring out what the synoptic Jesus (cf. Matthew 12:27; Luke 12:10) is saying by withholding forgiveness in this instance. In fact, discussions of the Markan version of this passage usually focus on the intercalated structure of the text, which allows for a broader view of the scene (i.e., how Jesus' harsh response to the scribes shapes our reading of his response to his family and how his final encounter with his family helps determine who is really Jesus' family). Kennedy turns our attention, though, to the scribes' harsh criticism of Jesus. Kennedy brings a response to the religious teachers by joining Mark 3 to Isaiah's suffering servant song, and in so doing, he deftly recovers collective and communal words that cross boundaries and draw people together.

In our own context, we are given numerous opportunities to divide ourselves. One of consumerism's greatest achievements is to offer sameness (market activity) under the guise of differentiation (freedom of choice). As such, my fashion preferences or food and drink choices become ample fodder for divisions and potential rivalry. Likewise, in the world of social media, a similar freedom is displayed in the simultaneous "likes" on Facebook and the tone-deaf judgmentalism that has become the speech-act *du jour*. Simply scanning one's news feed will reveal a host of variegated strong opinions but little that bridges gaps and brings people of disparate positions together. (One wonders whether Facebook's "Reactions" emoji will offer an improvement.) Across the board, the common, though not ubiquitous, result is fragmentation through condemnation and division.

Kennedy's sermon enters this space and asks where relationship lies, where community lies, and ultimately where the church lies. At first glance, his admonitions might be seen as only a critique of the "fire and brimstone" preaching that would be all too happy to label opponents (usually outsiders) as blasphemers and heretics. That is, those who oppose the gospel are blasphemers. In this passage, though, we need to notice that the "blasphemy against the Holy Spirit" that is the basis for the unforgivable sin seems to involve attributing the devil's activity to God's work. Rather than recognizing the power of the Holy Spirit in Jesus' ministry, the scribes say that "He has an unclean spirit" (Mark 3:30).

In commenting on the Markan passage, New Testament scholar David Garland states that many readers focus on the judgment without noticing the acceptance and forgiveness offered.[1] On a closer examination, then, Kennedy seems to be taking this road less traveled by focusing the earlier definition of blasphemy in a different location. In other words, Kennedy asks on what occasions we—rather than overt enemies of the gospel—become the blasphemers.

In a world where people have their pet causes and their inviolable principles, Kennedy notes that we sometimes "claim that our causes are the ways of the gospel." Indeed, this is true, and it is revealed in our pull toward quick and neat slogans that describe not only our own perspective but perhaps even provide the labels for our fellow brothers and sisters in Christ who disagree with us. Rhetorical opponents are described as evil, pagan, even non-Christian. When this happens, we begin to divide the community, and we are guilty of the same sort of blasphemy committed by the scribes.

In this sermon, then, Kennedy highlights the world depicted in the gospel as one shaped by the immense forgiveness offered by Jesus: "Truly I tell you, people will be forgiven for their sins and whatever blasphemies they utter" (Mark 3:28). This brings to mind another passage where forgiveness is prominently featured. In Matthew 18:21–22, Jesus responds to Peter's question about the frequency of forgiveness by saying, "Not seven

---

1. Garland, *The NIV Application Commentary: Mark*, 136.

times, but, I tell you, seventy times seven" (Matthew 18:22). In other words, forgiveness is to be a common characteristic of the followers of Jesus.

At one point, Kennedy states that "Baptists are not quite convinced about the power to forgive sins because we say only God can forgive sins. So Baptist pastors don't usually pronounce forgiveness of sins." He is certainly correct about this, but a bit more needs to be said. Whether spoken by a Catholic priest or a Baptist minister, the voice offering forgiveness speaks for the church, the pilgrim body of Christ in the world. Moreover, this is why such forgiveness is primarily offered in the context of liturgy. In fact, on the occasion of this sermon, a shared prayer of confession was spoken, followed by biblical words of assurance that the "God who is faithful and just" will forgive all our sins (1 John 1:9). This ecclesial act reminds us that confession and forgiveness requires a community in order to take root and grow.

Where the sermon might have been strengthened is in offering a more concrete vision of this alternative politics. That is, Kennedy opens with a scene from the television drama *Blue Bloods* where forgiveness is denied and retribution is sought. As Kennedy notes, we are familiar with this way of life. We know how the world is presently structured by violence, death, and even vengeance, but what does the eschatological vision of the kingdom of God look like when it breaks into our current reality? And what shape will our politics take then? One poignant counterexample might be the witness of the Amish of Nickel Mines, Pennsylvania, who forgave Charles Roberts, a man who shot ten Amish schoolgirls, ultimately killing five. The extent of the community's forgiveness (which included members attending Roberts' funeral and consoling his grieving family members) shocked the wider world as it shined a light on a different politics. While numerous examples could be offered, such events, which are certainly tragic, challenge the church to imagine a different way of performing the gospel. More importantly, by bringing about peace and reconciliation, they are acts that render ourselves whole and counter the rhetoric that divides the body of Christ.

Theologically speaking, Baptist theologian James McClendon has written that the creeds and confessional statements of the church "tell us how Scripture has been . . . read, and invite us to read it that way if we can.["2] With this in mind, we should remember the words of the Nicene Creed, that those who are bound together in Christ are "one, holy, catholic, ap-

---

2. McClendon Jr., *Doctrine*, 471.

ostolic church." In Acts 4, the boldness of the apostles is closely associated with their unity: "the whole group of those who believed were of one heart and soul" (Acts 4:32). Yet, we often view such boldness through the lens of "taking a stand" or being a prophetic lone ranger. With Kennedy's sermons in our ears, we might wonder whether the apostles' boldness was best manifested in their united life together. Moreover, we might consider whether we unwittingly violate a similar boldness by dividing Christ's body. After all, as Garland comments on the unforgivable sin, "Those who are probably most in danger of this sin today are the theologians, biblical experts, and leaders in the churches. They are also the most likely to level charges of blasphemy against others."[3]

Overall, Kennedy appropriately orients our vision to see the centrality of "our" and "we." These words challenge our individualized notions of sin and forgiveness and draw us toward the *corpus verum*—the true body of Christ. The Markan Jesus states, "If a kingdom is divided against itself, that kingdom cannot stand. And if a house is divided against itself, that house will not be able to stand (Mark 3:24–25). Indeed, John Howard Yoder has stated, "Where Christians are not united, the gospel is not true in that place."[4] Perhaps, then, instead of saying that the only unforgivable sin is "the refusal to ask for forgiveness," we might expand this to say that the only unforgivable sin is to refuse to be part of a people constituted by continual forgiveness and growing visible unity in love.

---

3. Garland, *The NIV Application Commentary: Mark*, 137.
4. Yoder, "The Imperative of Christian Unity," 391.

8

Sabbath Gospel
Mark 2:23–3:6

WHEN YOU HEAR THE word "Sabbath," I bet "gospel" is not the first word association you make. Let's see if Sabbath and gospel belong to one another. Like the Gospel, Sabbath is counterhistory, counterkingdom, counternation, countercommunity, and countereverything that matters so much to us that we practically worship them.

Paul Ricoeur said that obedience follows imagination. By that, I think he meant that our obedience will not venture far beyond or run risks beyond our imagined world. Before we could even attempt obedience to the Sabbath intended by God, we will need an enlightened, sanctified, baptized, imagination. Before we can do it, we must imagine it.

What would a present Kingdom of God, a life-style under God's direct dominion, look like? I want us to imagine a world that has evolved in answer to the prayer that Jesus taught us all to pray "Your kingdom come, your will be done, on earth as it is in heaven." The kingdom Jesus brings is unimaginable to us: non-violent, peaceful, enough for all.

Our lack of imagination has to do with what Walter Brueggemann labels the culture of now. The culture of now is a metaphorical construction mistaken for reality. Even the church has a vested interest that the way things are represent the way things should be. We have created a fake reality on an array of dominant metaphors and there are battalions of spokespersons daily supporting and defending the culture of now. The gods of exploitative systems go unchallenged and unnoticed. The abuse becomes normal. Investment firms budget for billions of dollars to be paid in fines in case they get caught breaking the law. It is known as the cost of doing business. Violence is unexamined as the cost of doing business. We are so numbed to Pharaoh's system that we have no idea how to enter into a Sabbath rest. Our motors are running for the next wild, tough, demanding scramble up the pyramid of the culture of now. We have to make more bricks.

And the message keeps pounding in our ears: More is better. Bigger is better. Violence is necessary. Punish our enemies. Don't let people push you around. Rich is better. Security is essential. Nationalism and capitalism matter most. America is God's favorite nation.

We are a nation built on falsehoods that are a blasphemy to the Gospel of Jesus Christ. I agree with the assessment of Ta-Nehisi Coates that the American dream is built on a lie. "This is the foundation of the Dream—its adherents must not just believe in it but believe that it is just, believe that their possession of the Dream is the natural result of grit, honor, and good works."[1] Our response has been to rewrite the Gospel so that it justifies the Dream as the entry into the Promised Land. Our inability to even imagine a culture without disproportion, war, violence, and greed indicates that the gospel falls on deaf ears. If only we could imagine the kingdom Jesus inaugurated.

There is a practice that is the advance guard of that world. That practice is Sabbath. The imagined world of Sabbath started at Sinai in Exodus 20. Sabbath is intended for all of creation. Paul says "We know that the whole creation has been groaning in labor pains until now."[2] Remember how the land was cursed after Eden. It is as if Sabbath begins to break the curse: "In the seventh year you shall let the land rest, so that the poor of your people may eat; and what they leave the wild animals may eat."[3]

The land gets a sabbatical. Our land, America could use a Sabbath. The 24/7 culture needs a break. The politics of destruction needs to zip it. The opinionators need a Sabbath. They need a day of silence every week with no one screaming. If they really believe what they are saying do they need to use that tone of voice? America—the land needs a Sabbath rest.

I once asked my father, "Do you think our mule looks forward to Sunday?" We plowed that mule Monday-Saturday from February to October.

---

1. Coates, *Between the World and Me*, 97.
2. Romans 8:22, *NRSV*.
3. Exodus 23:10–11, *NRSV*.

That mule didn't like to be plowed and I hated plowing that mule. As we made that last turn each day and headed for the barn, the mule would break into a trot, dragging plow and me all the way to the barn. Look, he knew. Even mules need a Sabbath.

Then over the centuries, the original Sabbath command of rest was re-interpreted in transforming ways. In Deuteronomy 5. Moses imagines Sabbath as freedom from Pharaoh's system. Moses says, "Remember the Exodus! Remember that the coercive system of Pharaoh was disrupted. Remember that the brick quota was declared null and void.

Why bring up Pharaoh? Well, Moses knew the temptation would be for the people to want to go back to Egypt. Moses cries out, "Remember what it was like when you had to make Pharaoh's bricks." Sabbath keeps us from being sucked into the vortex of restlessness. I fear for God's people who are returning to Egypt by deserting the church.

You may think that "Egypt" holds no sway over you. Let me ask: Do you worry that you do not meet expectations? That you don't always measure up? That you aren't making certain people happy? Worry that you aren't smarter or more successful? Do you think you are not good enough, not pretty enough, not talented enough? Do you lose sleep over not reaching your quota, your sales goals, your financial needs? Are you singing, "You can't buy much with the checks I'm cashing"? If this is your story, you have returned to Egypt.

The prophets have always been our most original spiritual imaginers. When Amos imagined Sabbath he saw a world where all disproportion had come to an end. Amos 8:4–6 gives Sabbath an economic reading, and asks us to imagine a world of economic justice. Amos says, "You sit in church and imagine new ways to cheat the poor." Amos imagines an end to disproportion but we find it unimaginable. It is inconceivable that a lower standard of living would be a blessing to the culture of now and more. Is it an indication of our spiritual poverty that we lack this imagination?

Turning now to the Gospel, we approach the most creative genius of imagination to ever live. "The Sabbath was made for human beings, not human beings for the Sabbath." Have we any idea of the universal application of this Jesus saying? No system is sacred. No institution is sacred. No nation is immune from judgment. Only human beings, created in God's image, are sacred. We don't work for institutions; institutions work for us.

Sabbath turns out to be good news. Turns out we need Sabbath as cure for our aggressive restlessness and personal loneliness. Stephen Hawking says that "aggression," humanity's greatest vice, will destroy civilization. He says that human beings continue to be stupidly aggressive—long after the evolutionary benefit of that kind of behavior has gone away. Sabbath gospel is for those who arrive here fatigued, anxious, desperately trying to be in control or at least appear to be in charge, desperate to have more control. We need to get our Sabbath practices back!

Sabbath is ordained into the very structure of created reality. On the seventh day God eased off daily management of creation and the world did not fall apart. In fact, it continued to evolve. The more robust the universe's creative economy is, the more the universe is indebted to its Creator for the richness of its existence. God gave the universe not just black holes, but a space that had zero anxiety. God was not a workaholic. God rested: confident, joyous, peaceful.

As disciples of Jesus, we can resist the culture of now with Sabbath practices that are not written into law but written on our hearts.

And of all things, on a Sabbath day, Jesus approaches a man with a withered hand. I see the man with the withered hand as a symbol of our culture. In Deuteronomy 15 Moses commands his people "do not be hard-hearted or tight-fisted towards your needy neighbor. ⁸You should rather open your hand, willingly lending enough to meet the need, whatever it may be." Moses knew that people would not naturally open their hands because of addiction to the Pharaoh system. What does this have to do with the man with the withered hand? The man with the withered hand could not open his hand to meet the needs of others. Then Jesus healed him and he stretched forth an open hand of gratitude and could then extend it to his neighbors in need. Sabbath creates people with open hands extended to others; not-Sabbath creates hard-hearted and tight-fisted persons.

I read a story of a refugee who walked seven hundred miles to escape a war. She walked all that way and brought with her an eight-year-old girl, who walked beside her. For seven hundred miles the child held her hand tightly. When they reached safety, the girl loosened her grip, and the woman looked at her hand. It was raw and bloody with an open wound, because the little girl had held on tightly in her fearfulness. When we extend our hand to the fearful, the restless, there can be no casual hand-holding.

Whose hands are free and whole to be extended to anyone? He who is the Sabbath extends his hand. "Come to me all you who are weary and are carrying heavy burdens, and I will give you rest. Take my yoke upon you, and learn from me; for I am gentle and humble in heart, and you will find rest for your souls."

Response
Sabbath Gospel

——— Mark Ryan ———

Words like "Sabbath" and "gospel" constitute a way of seeing, or learning to imagine, the world for Christians. We learn how to use these words, to live through them, by integrating our lives into the Christian narrative, where these words become intelligible. As Dr. Kennedy indicates in the second paragraph, our linguistically constituted *imagination* places limits around what we can see or experience. "Before we can do it, we must imagine it." In other words, our actions themselves take form in response to the worlds we imagine. So, the task of stretching the Christian imagination begins with attention to words.

Dr. Kennedy begins his diagnosis of the contemporary Christian imagination by suggesting, with Walter Brueggemann that we have been colonized by the "culture of now." The main purpose of this term seems to be to imply that we cannot see much beyond the way things are (as if we lived by the motto, "the way things are is the way things have to be.") But it also refers specifically to a modern, American life that is driven to create and consume whatever, to quote the title of a book by Michael Lewis on a restless silicon valley engineer/entrepreneur billionaire, is offered as the "new, new thing."

Dr. Kennedy turns to the way Moses re-interprets the command to keep the Sabbath in Deuteronomy 5. The command to keep the Sabbath as it is proclaimed in Exodus 20 puts the regulation in the context of Genesis

1 and its account of God's completion of creation. "For in six days the Lord made the heavens and the earth, the sea, and all that is in them, but he rested on the seventh day." (Ex. 20.11) We might say the stress here is in recognition of and allegiance to the one, true God, following immersion in a polytheistic society. In Deuteronomy 5, however, the background story is changed to the Exodus event, the liberation of the Israelites from Pharaoh's rule. "Remember that you were slaves in Egypt and that the Lord your God brought you out of there with a mighty hand and an outstretched arm." (Deut. 5:15) Dr. Kennedy exploits this narrative shift to reason that Moses was now well aware that the Israelite's would be tempted to return to the system of Pharaoh. The seeds of a new slavery, we might say, were being carried around within them. Some years ago, perhaps nearer to the time of the inception of the current competitive circuit—which, causing players to lead a life of travel round the world, and taking a break for only about 3 weeks in December—I read an interview in which a player referred to the computerized ranking system as "that unforgiving, bitch goddess." Ways in which society attributes worth to human beings really do come to rule over us, going beyond whatever professed usefulness they were created for.

I think this gives a different inflection to the sermon theme of the Sabbath as an alternative reality that requires transcending the culture of now. Pointing to the frenetic, and chaotic, way we live and asserting that our outlook needs transcending in order for the kingdom to come into view is not false, yet it may cause us to have a false sense of confidence about our knowledge of where we are and what is to be done to make things better. The new inflection stemming from Moses's insight that the Israelites themselves are tempted to return to Egypt is in a way more subtle; it implies that the Israelites (and we, ourselves, by extension) likely need to be made aware that they are at risk of becoming slaves again, and perhaps already are in the grips of tyranny.

Thus, Dr. Kennedy here enters an "ad hominem" rhetorical mode, raising a series of questions designed to get his audience to make a connection of which they are currently unaware. "Do *you* worry that you do not meet expectations? That you aren't making certain people happy? Worry that you aren't smarter or more successful?" The ad hominem turn is fitting because at this point because the speaker's purpose is to get his audience to make a connection they have not yet made: to think on the spot and, indeed, to stretch their imaginations.

The word "metanoia" in Greek seems to mean "turning around" and is translated "conversion." Perhaps where we put our attention is simpler way to think of it. One of the ways the principalities of this world, what Dr. K alludes to as "the culture of now," garner our worship is through capturing our attention. Think of the things we obsess about, as Dr. K just invited us to do.[1] These thoughts and preoccupations and worries do not merely reflect our allegiances, but I would say also partly constitute them. We all like to think that, though we're just like most anybody else at work, in trying to be shrewd as serpents about politics, in appearing competent, polished, perhaps unproblematic ("smooth") in our performances before colleagues, we nevertheless would never find ourselves being caught off-guard by a scandalous dilemma.[2] But the truth seems to be that what really shapes us morally is where our attention typically resides much of the time, during ordinary life. What we may think of as "mere distractions" or as "important, but not centrally important" or "my work life but not who I, authentically, am" actually represent the pharaoh under whose power we dwell, even "our god."

---

1. A student, with whom I'd had a conference during the last month of class about his final paper draft, handed it in to me at the end of our last class. As he did so, he apologized for the way he reacted to the constructive criticism I'd given him at the conference. He explained that he'd been having a bad day and just couldn't stomach any kind critique. A week ago, after the grades were in, the apology took on a new light. What I realized—he was one of just 4 students in the seminar, so it was easy to tell—is that he had taken out his hurt in the student evaluation he wrote. I mention this because, when I think of this sometimes even now, I wince about the way he lowered my scores. Even knowing the whole story, I can't help obsessing with the scores!

2. In a really serious matter, involving profound moral matters, we would flee from evil; we would not succumb to compromising with it or endangering the fragile inner sanctum of our consciences. Perhaps we envision fleeing at such a moment to FBC, whose walls we imagine can't be penetrated by evil.

In the noonday devotion in the *Book of Common Prayer* one finds the following verse: "O Lord, you will keep in perfect peace those whose minds are fixed on you. In returning and rest we shall be saved, in quietness and trust shall be our strength." I like the association here between meditation on God and rest. It reminds me of the metaphysical meditations of Christian philosopher like Boethius, who practiced such meditation while exiled and imprisoned on false charges.

To be able to find "rest" has been a very important topic for me for some years, especially while working. In my case, it is not because I am conscientious to point of working long hours, or have such a hectic schedule I am up till late at night. The problem is more subtle: insomnia. While I was trying to get my dissertation going some 9 years ago in Charlottesville, VA, I had my first night where I just never quite did go to sleep. A terrifying novelty! I've never been a terrific sleeper—the kind who can drift off to sleep with five minutes on her hands during a bus ride—but since I could remember a certain amount of sleep came to me eventually each and every night of my life. Since then, I've struggled. How much of the change is really a physiological and how much is psychological is difficult to say.

As a sufferer of insomnia, I became the victim of a fuzzy sort of problem. The "fuzziness" comes from the varying antidotes applied to it. On one hand, there is no shortage of medical and psychological experts on the topic—of hi tech pharmaceuticals designed to fix it at a stroke. Yet, if we are honest, it remains unclear just what sort of problem it is. Is it physical? (You can have a sleep study done for a few grand.) s it psychological? (I myself participated in a clinical trial through a large university hospital's department of behavioral medicine.) Is it spiritual? (Think of the semi-quackery in the spiritual remedies being sold.)

But I think a real key to the sort of problem is found in the new identity—i.e., victim—that it gives to its sufferers. In many ways I think this ailment feeds upon a shaping of character that flows from a new narrative. As we saw above, narratives shape a person's sense of self, and the story of suffering, which began for me with that initial shock and disorientation of not being able to sleep can mold one's vision of one's abilities, one's prospects, one's possible future. (Lord be with us in such moments of extreme vulnerability!)

Other stories rise up to combat the feeling of vulnerability produced by suffering. Stories of heroic resistance, self-power and new and stronger forms of being are plentiful. Such stories often have mottos, i.e. "Boston Strong."

Rod's sermon enters this agon of stories not as its own (competing) offer of a straightforward 'fix,'[3] but rather as an alternative interpretation of ourselves. It is, moreover, a story or interpretation meant to unveil the other stories for what they are: partial truths which easily lead to their own forms of enslavement. In particular, I claim that the sermon intends to show how these stories, linked as they are to the culture of continual productivity, so shape our imaginations as to keep us squarely in the culture of now—i.e. restless.

The Sermon as Sacrament

All of this perhaps brings us round again to the theme of Dr.. Kennedy's sermon. We might put it in the form of a question, what is the task of the Christian imagination? I would like to try and get at this by reflecting on something Dr Kennedy often says about the nature and purpose of sermons—namely, their "sacramental" character.

Theologian Herbert McCabe explains the nature of sacraments by analogy with the political cartoon. Such representations of policies and politicians have the character of a "creative interpretation" of actual policies and politicians. By highlighting some particular aspect of that law or figure, typically through exaggeration, they invite viewers to reinterpret them and light of the highlighted feature. McCabe notes that we often produce such an image of ourself, one which allows us to (re)interpret who we are. He continues, "such an image is a realization of ourselves in two possible senses of the word: it is both a recognition of who and what we are and also a making real of who and what we are."[4]

Sacraments, then dwell at the border of the already and not yet. They reflect the tension between the present and the future; indeed, they make the future, after a fashion, present. They do so by allowing the not yet to reinterpret they already, and draw the latter toward it. "The sacramental life is the creative interpretation of the world in terms of the presents to it of Christ, its future."

---

3. I admit, during a particular spell of poor sleep, to keeping the sermon on my nite table and looking it over before laying down for the night.

4. McCabe, *Law, Love, and Language*, 143.

If the Sunday sermon is part of the church's sacramental life, it must have a part in creatively interpreting the world in which we live in terms made available by its future: Christ. Thus, a sermon that proclaims the way things are is the way they must be is by definition a poor sermon—a failed attempt at sacramentality, we might say. We should, by contrast, find a good sermon a little difficult to believe; that is, because it is not reflecting back to us but we simply know as truth. and yet, we should also find it compelling, having some sense that the world of which it speaks is being made real in our presence.

The creative interpretation of the church's present in light of its future is unveiled as a captivity to the culture of now. This might be humiliating but it is good news in a way. For captivity to the "culture of now" is importantly different from simple immersion in that culture. That is, describing it as "captivity" means the church has the power to begin to free itself: knowing what captivity looks like, here and now, is the first step.

Another way to put this, I would say, is that good sermons help us and that ongoing struggle to give ourselves to the gospel. This, to give ourselves to the gospel, seems to me a fitting description of the end of the Christian imagination. Through creatively interpreting us to ourselves, by the use of images, stories, arguments, humor and more, the sermon helps us to resist are unimaginative captivity to the culture of now. It does so by allowing us not merely to glimpse but abide a while in the future which is the gospel.

As I claimed earlier, but now for us is composed of a vision of self in relation to the world and God. To be enslaved in Egypt is to be caught in the image of humanity as independent from God's story. In creatively reinterpreting us to ourselves, the sermon challenges and resists that vision of ourselves which is our captivity. It helps to free us *from* the technologies of restlessness, and free us *for* true rest. The liberation of our imagination is something like what Jesus asks us to do, when he says come to me, all who are weary and heavy laden

9

Welcome to the Family
Mark 3:31–35

JESUS HAS CREATED A new kind of family where we are all brothers and sisters. There's a Cajun song that tells you about the four ways to become a Cajun: you can be born one, marry one, get one to adopt you, or come in the back door. Well, we don't get to choose our biological family, but we can become part of another family—the family of God. Now, there are some folks with some pretty harsh understandings about being part of God's family. I read where someone asked, "Why does the church let sin come in the back door?" The implication was that the church is a place of holiness and that the church should be guarding all the doors to keep sin out. How odd that a congregation of sinners would be worrying about the back door when sin walks right in the front door every Sunday morning. Overall, I think there is too much gnashing of teeth and wringing of hands over the sins of others especially given our inability to actually identity at times what is and what is not sinful behavior.

Family vocabulary is rather complicated isn't it? On a personal level I hear a lot of folks say, "I love the sinner but hate the sin." If this is a genuine expression of your relationship with another person and you truly love them, that is one thing, but as a blanket statement it is a way of using love as a weapon of condemnation. We are sneaky with our language and can cloak our worst actions in the protest of love at times like an abusive husband crying, "I only hit you because I love you." Reinhold Niebuhr once remarked, we are "never as dangerous as when we act in love," for then we are at our worst as judges of what we are actually doing.

Some Christians don't like the terms "brothers and sisters" because they connect it to a kind of backwoods ignorance, but it is deeply intimate, New Testament, Christian language. When I am afforded the privilege of preaching in African American churches, the pastor usually introduces me as his other brother from another mother. I am not sure what that means other than the pastor likes the rhythm and rhyme of the words and that he is genuinely welcoming me as a member of his family.

I am suggesting that Jesus welcomes all who are willing to join his family. He says, "Here are my mother and my brothers! ³⁵Whoever does the will of God is my brother and sister and mother." I'm hanging my hat on these beautiful words. The "whoever" there may or may not be a bunch of Christians. And he says, "Listen! I am standing at the door, knocking; if you hear my voice and open the door, I will come in to you and eat with you, and you with me." God lets people in through all the doors of heaven. According to John's Revelation there are twelve doors/gates into heaven. Even if the people who came through door number one think they are the only ones in heaven, they have no idea how many of us came through the back door.

There is, however, something unsettling about this claim that we are members of God's family and it has to do with the pronouns, especially "we." Barbara Brown Taylor said that the first day that she taught a college class and said the words, "We believe": "I saw a look pass over the face of a young man named Kamal that let me know my *we* was too small for him. Later I would learn that he was a Hindu from Sri Lanka who had lots of practice with pronouns snapping shut on him. On the first day, all I knew was that my language had left him out."[1] Isn't it sad that "we Christians" have invented so many ways to shut people out? Our language can be condescending, off-putting. George Steiner claims that all language is designed for self-protection. Paul Tournier, a Swiss doctor and psychiatrist always said that we all accuse and we all defend. Christians are experts of putting people in what communication scholar Deborah Tannen calls a "one-down position." You can't build yourself up by putting other people down. "I thank you that I am not like other people: thieves, rogues, adulterers, or even like this tax collector." It seems that for every Christian working for unity, for ecumenical spirit, for the catholic spirit of our faith there are a

---

1. Taylor, *Leaving Church*, 207.

thousand closing doors, throwing up doctrinal and liturgical walls. How big is the "we" in your vocabulary?

The other children of Mary had issues with their brother. These are not Jesus' cousins or children of Joseph by another marriage. Mark says that the family of Jesus tried to put him under house arrest. Remember the nonsense song: Peter, Peter pumpkin eater had a wife and couldn't keep her so he put her in a pumpkin shell and there he kept her very well. Well, Jesus had a disciple named Peter and he was always trying to get Jesus to settle down in one place. Peter tried to keep Jesus as his house in Capernaum and on the Mount of Transfiguration Peter wanted to build a gated community and keep Jesus there. Dominic Crossan suggests that Peter saw the opportunity for Jesus to be the "patron" and Peter his "broker." The idea of locking Jesus into one system, one house is always our temptation. My cousin Boudreaux says, "Jesus may have other sheep in other flocks, but I don't have to accept them." But you can't keep Jesus in a house made with hands, not in Peter's house at Capernaum, not even in Peter's house in Rome.

Mark consistently shows the family and the disciples either not understanding Jesus or trying to block his road to the cross. Dominic Crossan suggests that the family of Jesus did believe in his power and importance, message and mission, but not in the way he was carrying it out. His family thought that Jesus should settle down in Nazareth, and establish there a healing cult. That would have worked for Jesus' family and for little Nazareth itself. Dayton has the Wright Brothers. Nazareth would have Jesus. One problem: Jesus refused to hang out his shingle as resident doctor.

Our desire to build a house to keep our religious experience is not wrong, but it can become wrong. A church built only as a monument to the past is well on its way to becoming a museum. Carlyle Marney said, "It was so with Moses, David, Solomon, Muhammed, Simon Peter, Joseph Smith." Look, everybody's got houses for God but no guarantee that God will stay. God will not stay where God is not wanted, worshiped, and proclaimed. God will leave dead churches, hang a wreath on the door, and put a FOR SALE sign in the yard. Marney reminds us that a house to the Lord arose in Shiloh. Then they learned that some days God didn't come to church. They had real estate but no God they could guarantee to inhabit it. So the house fell down. The glory of the Lord departed and the Lord came no more to Shiloh.[2] No matter how frenetic the activity or the multiplicity of

---

2. Marney, "A Come and Go Affair," 135.

the programs or the excitement of the music a church can have a name that it is alive and be "deader than a door nail."

What about us? Do we want Jesus as our house doctor or the savior of the world? If so we have made a common mistake in reading the gospel as being primarily about personal salvation and thinking that the primary question is "Are you saved?" I believe that we are part of a family that transcends the "current fascination with individual salvation in both liberal and conservative guises."[3] I assume that salvation is about us being engrafted into a family with practices that save us from those powers that would rule our lives.

When Christians say that blood is thicker than water we are saying that the blood of Jesus has made us all members of his family. The blood of Christ has made us all one family. Paul says in Romans 5, "Therefore just as one man's trespass led to condemnation for all, so one man's act of righteousness leads to justification and life for all."[4] They nailed Jesus to a cross because he refused to be nailed down by the expectations, desires, false hopes, wishes, crazy nationalistic dreams of other people. Refusing to be boxed in by his family, Jesus went out into the world. Dominic Crossan calls it radical itinerancy.

If you want to follow Jesus, welcome to the family. No ifs, ands, or buts, just welcome to the family. If you will do the will of God, welcome to the family. Let me see if I can illustrate this with a story from history. On Christmas Eve, 1814, the British came up the Mississippi River to attack New Orleans. Andrew Jackson was the commander of the American force. When General Jackson realized that he lacked enough soldiers to resist the British attack, he recruited people from all ranks of life including the infamous pirate Jean Lafitte and his nefarious crew. Faced with imminent danger and defeat, Jackson forgot protocol, distinctions, and invited anyone who could hold a gun or a sword to help defend New Orleans. If you would like to be a member of the family of Jesus, you are invited. You can be born into this family through new birth; you can be adopted into this family by the grace of God; you can be baptized into this family; you can even come in the back door. In George McDonald's story *The Princess and the Goblin*, Curdie, a strapping young miner, has been captured by goblins and is trapped in a cave. One night little Irene, hearing goblins in her house, takes out a magic thread given to her by her fairy grandmother and starts to

---

3. Hauerwas, *In Good Company*, 8.
4. Romans 5:18, *NRSV*.

follow it. It takes her into the darkness she dreads, but she follows it in faith, finds Curdie, and leads him out. But Curdie can't see or feel the thread. He tells Irene, "I am very grateful that you saved my life, but I don't believe in your grandmother or the thread." Vexed, she protests, "How could I have ever saved you without the thread?" When Irene's fairy grandmother appears next, she says, "He is a good boy, Curdie, and a brave boy. Aren't you glad you have got him out?"

"Yes, Grandmother," says Irene, "but it wasn't very good of him not to believe me when I was telling him the truth." Now, what the grandmother says next is important to us: "People must believe what they can, and those who believe more must not be hard upon those who believe less. I doubt you have believed it all yourself if you hadn't seen some of it." This, in story, is my message: People who believe more must not be hard on those who believe less. And I want to add a second layer of meaning: People who believe more must not be hard on those who believe differently.

Let's suppose that we are willing to give this new family of Jesus some real life around here. If you get with people who are trying to do the will of God and work with them, you will find your way to Jesus. That's where he hangs out with his family: The family of those who do God's will. That is why we pray every time we gather: Your kingdom come, your will be done on earth as it is in heaven. Amen.

Response
Welcome to the Family

 Brad J. Kallenberg _____

In his sermon, "Welcome to the Family" (22 Mar 2015), Rod Kennedy observes that there is "something unsettling about [the] claim that we are members of God's family, and it has to do with the pronouns, especially 'we.'" Answering the question "Who is the 'we'?" is as contentious an issue as can be found. For some people there are *practical* difficulties: "If a wall required to keep out the Mexicans, then should the Mexican government be made to pay for it?"[1] For others *ethical* difficulties are paramount: "Is it a duty or merely a right for us to water our lawns in time of severe drought?"[2] Lurking behind these and other pressing issues are *conceptual* difficulties. I want briefly to consider the last problem by comparing three different ways to approach delineating corporate identity.

One way of designating corporate identity, of naming the "we," can be understood on the model of a barrier.[3] A fence is a good example. I put up a fence around my garden to keep the critters out. Prisons build fences and walls to keep the bad people in. In both cases the intention is clear: to separate one group (the "good") from another (the "bad"). Even when the barrier does not prevent crossing over (e.g., railroad tracks, a river, a

---

1. Primack, "Donald Trump's Plan to Pay for Mexico Border Wall."
2. Rory Carroll, "California Drought Threatens."
3. Agam-Segal, "Contours and Barriers."

highway), the effective designation of the population into "them" and "us" is unmistakable.

As is well known, the Barrier Model often turns on the application of very specious criteria for classifying groups. For example, designations have been made solely on the basis of phenotypic properties (skin color, eye color, hair color, width of the nose, height-to-weight ratio, etc.).[4] Likewise, socially-conditioned metrics are sometimes used. Features such as *language, dialect, accent* (in Judges 12:6 the imposters couldn't pronounce "Shibboleth"; in Mt 26:73 Peter is betrayed by his Galilean accent), *etiquette, customs*, even *food preferences* have also been used to parse people groups. Today we are willing to surrender specious criteria on the assumption that DNA sequencing will reliably tell us which people go into which groups.[5] Whether DNA can bear this weight is disputable.[6] My point is only that DNA functions as a Barrier Model.

The Barrier Model of social identity can be found at work in both testaments. In the Hebrew Bible, Jeremiah warns inhabitants of Jerusalem that it is no used comforting themselves with the mantra "This is the temple of the Lord, the temple of the Lord, the temple of the Lord" (Jer. 7:4) because the invading Babylonians would be unstoppable. Why did Israel think the temple might save them? Because they thought YHWH was tethered *to the temple*.

A series of ambiguous verses in the Hebrew Bible refer to "the center of the earth."[7] When the Israelites conquered Canaan, they retained cultural

---

4. Often phenotypic properties lie on a smooth continuum. For example, Brazilians use 134 different terms to self-describe their skin colors! Under these conditions, cut-offs are determined by fiat. Infamously King Leopold II of Belgium divided Rwandan peoples into Hutus from Tutsis on artificial criteria and granted the taller, whiter, and thinner-nosed Tutsis wealth, privilege and power to rule the shorter, thicker, wide-nosed Hutus. The formerly peaceful Rwandans have been warring ever since. See Emmanuel Katongole, *The Sacrifice of Africa: A Political Theology for Africa*, 1–25. On complex racial identity in Brazil see Lourdes Garcia-Navarro, "Dark-Skinned or Black? How Afro-Brazilians Are Forging a Collective Identity," *All Things Considered* (12 Aug 2015). http://www.npr.org/sections/codeswitch/2015/08/12/431244962/dark-skinned-or-black-how-afro-brazilians-are-forging-a-collective-identity.

5. The family of former President William Harding have recently been forced to admit that James Blaesing is a bona fide grandson through Harding's mistress Nan Britton. Bill Chappell, "Warren Harding, We Hardly Knew Ye," ibid. (13 Aug 2015). http://www.npr.org/sections/thetwo-way/2015/08/13/432064123/warren-harding-we-hardly-knew-ye.

6. See current research on epigenomics, the field that studies the causal connections between genes and the local physical environment.

7. Judges 9:37; Psalm 74:12; Isaiah 2:2 & 14:13; Ezekiel 5:5 & 38:12.

awareness of "The Myth of Omphalos." Omphalos was the cosmic navel, the single location where heaven, earth and the underworld converged. It was marked and sealed by a great stone. Solomon shrewdly placed his Temple there and the site, formerly called Mt. Moriah, became known as Mt Zion ever since.[8] Apparently Jeremiah's peers thought they were safe because unlike the Babylonians, "they" were the ones on *this* side of the barrier, on this side of Omphalos. (Note: Things didn't work out so well for them.)

Likewise, the NT recounts the painful—but unanimous—decision to let non-Jews into the Christian church (with certain provisos; Acts 15). Later Paul would insist that the problem faced in Acts 15 was a pseudo-problem, because all such barrier metrics were pseudo-criteria; not one of them picked out a property of genuine significance: "There is no longer Jew or Greek, there is no longer slave or free, there is no longer male and female; for all of you are one in Christ Jesus" (Gal 3:28).

A second model might be called Centripetal. If a Barrier Model of identity functions on the basis of exclusion, the Centripetal model forms groups by means of their attraction and proximity to a center. We can keep toddlers in the park by means of a sturdy fence. But toddlers might also be corralled without a fence, by simply putting ice cream and puppies in their midst!

Philosopher Gary Mar once observed that Asian cultures tend to understand Christianity centripetally. For example, a Korean painting of the Sermon on the Mount shows Jesus seated on a hillside, surrounded by roughly concentric rings of listeners. The path winds up the mountain in almost spiral fashion. In Asian eyes, comments Mar, the question is not who is "in" or who is "out"—a quintessentially Western way to see matters—but how close is one to the center (aka Jesus) and in which direction is one moving (toward or away from the center)?[9]

---

8. 2 Chronicles 3:1 and 1 Chron. 21:18–22. The cult of Omphalos was typified by snake worship, sun-worship, and primal waters. Solomon's Temple was (1) oriented toward the sunrise and (2) has in the front an enormous "Sea of Bronze," which is reminiscent of the primal waters of both Jewish creation story (Gen 1:1–2) and other ANE chaos mythologies. In addition, (3) the innermost room of Solomon's Temple was sometimes called the *debir* (1 Kings 6:5), a word related to "oracle" (as in "the Oracle of Delphi"). The similarities are too striking to be accidental. One source puts it this way: " . . . Solomon's temple is built on a rock which is the earth-center, the world-mountain, the foundation stone of creation, the extremity of an umbilical chord . . . a link between heaven, earth and the underworld." Samuel Terrien, "The Omphalos Myth and Hebrew Religion," 317.

9. Mar, "Evangelization through Asian Eyes.".

The advantage of the Centripetal Model over the Barrier Model is at least three-fold. First, the Centripetal Model is more realistic in that it admits of a sliding scale rather than clear cutoffs. Second, the Centripetal Model is simpler. It only needs to keep track of one item, and this item is common to all: the center. This feature better fits the emphasis of Christianity that Jesus is the only one that matters; "He must increase, but we must decrease" (Jn. 3:30). Third, the Centripetal Model may be emergent rather than imposed. Thus it functions entirely naturally. Without any external coercion (though such coercion *was* supplied), immigrants naturally tended to congregate and live in close proximity to others who spoke their language, ate similar food, and so on.

The third model for thinking about corporate identity might be called the Contour Model. In contrast to the former two, the Contour Model tolerates more ambiguity "out there" while increasing the demands "in here." I mean that Barrier and Centripetal Models are "objective" in the sense that the metrics and/or the center can be specified at a distance, from *outside* the population in question. But the Contour Model involves you and me as insiders, as human subjects who must truthfully face our skills or lack thereof.

Like all people, we tend to fear ambiguity. To the extent we hold power in social environments (say over one's children or over one's employees or classroom), we invent rules and procedures to keep things within the ambit of predictability and control. The more black and white, the better. When things begin turning grey, the tendency is to add yet another layer of regulation. However, most of our lives are lived in ambiguity.

Is it ever obvious precisely where a valley ends and the hillside begins? Or if I say, "Stand roughly there," is not the average person able to comply despite the ambiguity of "roughly"? Will specifying the spot to the nearest foot make the command clearer? To the nearest millimeter? To the nearest nanometer?! "Is it even always an advantage to replace an indistinct picture by a sharp one? Isn't the indistinct one often exactly what we need?"[10] We learn to apply the concept of "valley" by being able to read the contours of the landscape. If I am the sort who feels unsure where the valley is until it can be marked by a line the width of a human hair, I then would *not* know where the valley was, because *I would not yet know how to use the word "valley"* like everyone else. The problem is not with imprecise definition but with my lack of fluency. The skill of reading contours must be learned,

---

10. Wittgenstein, *Philosophical Investigations*, §71.

whether those contours were of actual landscapes or of grammatical ones. And learning such skill requires training over time. In short, it requires discipleship.

Nothing can be as countercultural as conceptual differences. Native Americans offered goodwill gifts to the European settlers of the so-called "New World." In doing so, they expected those gifts to be passed on. When the Europeans simply kept them, they eventually asked for the gifts back, fearing the "storm damage" that was sure to follow from insulting the deity that inhabited the gift. Gifts, by their definition, *must keep moving*. The Europeans, of course, thought of gifts in line with private property, as *something to hoard*, and began slandering their new neighbors as "Indian Givers."[11] The distance between the two cultures couldn't be farther precisely because those differences were conceptual.

Rod Kennedy's preaching is countercultural to the extent that he exposes conceptual differences. Western culture is obviously rife with the Barrier Model determining who's "in" and who's "out." But Christianity has rejected all the metrics—"there is no longer Jew or Greek, there is no longer slave or free, there is no longer male and female." When Kennedy observes that Jesus' family would have been happy had Jesus settled down and hung out his shingle in Nazareth, he is showing the Centripetal Model is also too small for Christianity. But employing a Contour Model comes at the price of "radical itinerancy."

---

11. The earliest use of the term seems to be Thomas Hutchinson's history of the Puritan colony ca. 1764. My understanding of gift economies is derived almost entirely from Lewis Hyde's important extension of Marcel Mauss's original study by the same title; see Hyde, *The Gift*, 3–142, esp. 3–31.

10

Are American Christians Persecuted?
Mark 6:14–29, Matthew 5:10–16

Jesus says, "Blessed are the persecuted." Anyone here saying, "I got to get me some of that?" Do you believe Christians are being persecuted in America? A lot of Christians believe this narrative about persecution. It comes in the colorful gift wrapping of religious liberty. Let's unwrap this narrative package, and see if Christians are being persecuted. Conspiracy theories are a growth industry in America. To paraphrase Kurt Cobain, of the rockband Nirvana, "Just because you are paranoid doesn't mean they're not after you."

I'm sure you read the story from Bastrop, Texas. The US Army scheduled a drill there and the word went out that the US Army was invading Texas to take away their guns, and lock all the citizens in abandoned Wal Mart stores. Conspiracy theories used to be fun hobby for some folks. Now, they are just plain dangerous. You just never know when you will wake up one morning and discover that TV news has baked your brain and you will think Jesus is coming back at noon, that the army is coming for your family, and that you are going to be arrested for standing up for your Christian convictions.

There is so much mistrust in America that in many Christian circles, the more credentials you have, the less likely you are to be believed. Millions of Americans trust the word of Ken Ham at the Creation Museum over the most important scientists in the world. Millions more trust the word of David Barton, who does revisionist history as a hobby over the conclusions of the most respected historians in the world. Barton believes all the Founding Fathers were born again Christians; that Thurgood Marshall should be left out of history textbooks, and the First Amendment is a lie of the devil. He wrote a book, *The Lies of Jefferson*, and it was so riddled with his own fabrications of the sayings of our founding fathers that the publisher took the unprecedented step of removing the book from all bookstores. It turns out the book was riddled with the lies of David Barton. "I disagree with these experts" has become the new American mantra. The insights of the unschooled, under-educated are often more valued than those of credentialed, experienced experts.

There is a media narrative that Christians are being persecuted. I believe that "narratives" are more important than isolated "texts" or verses of Scripture. It is not good exegesis to isolate a single verse of Scripture and then treat it as if it contains all the truth. It is also not helpful to do this with one book of the Bible. A person fixated on Genesis (Can you say, "Ken Ham"?) or on Revelation will have a skewered world vision. If we read the "narratives" of Scripture—our stories, we will find out who we are, what is expected of us, and what we are supposed to be doing as the disciples of Jesus. Knowing "our" story we will be less likely to fall victim to false narratives. This is especially important in light of the demonic dualisms currently in vogue in so many conservative circles. Preachers want us to believe that we must be for or against this or that issue or something is wrong with our Christianity. The claim is simply false. Don't fall into the trap of dualism.

Always keep in mind that television only appears to be all-powerful and all-knowing. Television universalizes a single example. Don't universalize one example of alleged persecution into the marching of armies of persecutors into our churches. In the discipline of rhetoric, this is known as hasty generalization and is a major fallacy in many arguments. In fact, argument in America has so degenerated that it is now better known for its fallacies than its factuality: scapegoating, personal attacks, guilt by association, and fear tactics. Aristotle must be furious. But my use of rhetorical principles, according to the anti-intellectual standard in America, should be discounted because I have a Ph.D. in rhetoric and have spent my life studying the nature and impact of argument and persuasion on audiences. The late 19th and early 20th century produced a mythology that an educated clergy would destroy the church. A popular evangelist hooted, "We

ARE AMERICAN CHRISTIANS PERSECUTED?

have been clamoring for fifty years for an educated ministry and we have got it to-day, and the church is deader than it ever has been in its history. Educated preachers are little more than the sum of their degrees: "A.B.'s, Ph.D's, D.D's; and A.S.S's"[1]

This myth overlooks the fact that the first centuries of the church was filled with the most highly educated members of society, and that the church has always valued higher education. We invented the university and served as the incubator for Western science. Those of us who support education as vital to the church are caught between the conservative mistrust of education and the secular disdain for Christianity. The conservatives think we are too smart to be trusted; the secularists that we are not smart at all. There is the sense that everyone who's anyone (smart people who are not religious who went to good schools that used to be religious) is smarter than any person of faith. What's a preacher to do?

I can only go on as before—attempting to use my acquired skills to argue as persuasively as possible for alternatives. So, here's my argument: no matter what you are hearing, no preachers are going to be arrested after their sermons this morning. Nobody listens to pulpit sermons any more in the first place. Nobody is going to lynch, drown, or burn a preacher at the stake. Preachers are a protected species in America. Congregations will put up with bad preaching for years and every Sunday, people will mumble, "Nice sermon, Rev." And they will say, "He's such a nice little preacher." We have housing allowances, tax exemptions, and invitations to all the right social events, especially if a prayer is needed. I was on the Miami Valley Foundation Board for 8 years and my primary function was to pray at board lunch meetings. They never asked me how to invest their $125 million and that's smart. I have been praying for my dinner for five decades, but have never been persecuted. Criticized but not persecuted.

What is persecution? Historically, persecution has meant imprisonment, floggings, drownings, beheadings, crucifixions, murders, and martyrdom. Ask the Anabaptists. Ask the Jews, but don't ask spoiled, pampered, soft American Christians growling about their rights. Around the world, there is real persecution of Christians. There are 28 countries currently on the persecution watch list; the USA is not one of those countries. Christians in Bethlehem have either been killed or chased out of town. In Israel, Christians are persecuted by the ultra-Orthodox—the super religious Jews. It is

---

1. Stephens and Giberson, *The Anointed*, 8.

a sad fact of history that religious fundamentalists of all stripes are more likely to engage in persecution than unbelievers.

For Christians, the Bible remains the go-to reference for helping us negotiate the world around us. I am not talking about a verse from here and there and pretending that the entire faith of the Christian world hangs on the literal reading of that verse. Not all texts are faith-bearing words. I once wanted to remodel an apartment by removing a wall. The contractor came, took a look, and said, "I can take out that wall because it is not a load-bearing wall." The same is true of the Bible.

The story from Mark's gospel today is a story of the persecution of John the Baptist. Now this is real persecution. John must tell Herod that it is a sin that he has taken away his brother's wife and married her. A king who knows no restraint, who doesn't play according to God's book, has to be told there is an unmovable truth in the Word of God that cannot be violated. John was arrested for telling the king the truth. And then beheaded. Real persecution.

And then there's the direct teaching of Jesus. In our reading from the Sermon on the Mount, Jesus says, "Blessed are those who are persecuted for righteousness' sake, for theirs is the kingdom of heaven." Then he says, "Love your enemies and pray for those who persecute you." In Luke 21:12–19 Jesus expands his teaching on how Christians are to respond to persecution. "This will give you," Jesus says, "an opportunity to testify."

Persecution is a blessing. You probably have to be an Anabaptist to think like this. I fear that we have lost the spirit of Jesus, that we have banished him to the wilderness of our secular concrete jungles. We know we are in trouble when the teaching of Jesus makes no sense to us—when we are turned off by the idea of loving enemies, being persecuted for righteousness sake, and praying for those who persecute us. Will it dawn on us at some point that when we don't get the teaching of Jesus we don't get Jesus no matter how "saved" and "born again" we think we are? If we don't practice what Jesus taught us, then I must tell you that our salvation is at least questionable.

It turns out that we are not being persecuted; we are under pressure. If you have faith today you are faced with a relentless and often unspoken pressure. Our faith stances are contested and strange, maybe even preposterous or unimaginable in a secular culture. No wonder we are so reluctant to speak of Jesus in public. There is the sense that the secular world is a cool, monolithic, rational age where everyone who's anyone (smart people who are not religious who went to good schools that used to be religious) lives in quiet confidence. This is the pressure that we face and it is not persecution but it is more dangerous.

There is immense pressure to give up Christianity because it is not smart enough or tough enough. And many of the converts to unbelief talk about "growing up" and "facing reality"—painting faith as immature and childish."

Christians facing actual persecution have a different spirit than the one American Christians are showing. In Will Campbell's novella, *Cecelia's Sin*, we are given a moving picture of three Anabaptists preparing to face death as martyrs. Here is what the true spirit of persecuted Christians who are following Jesus' teachings actually looks like. Cecelia gathers all her possessions the night before her arrest in order to give them away. She will be dispossessed of her possessions willingly. She says, "These must be distributed before they come. The sentence will call for the confiscation of all my possessions. If I give them away before they come they are no longer my possessions." That is the spirit of Jesus.

Cecelia begins to pray aloud: "Grace, joy, and peace from God the heavenly Father, and our Lord Jesus Christ, who loved us, and washed us from our sins in his own blood, and hath shined bright in our hearts, and translated us into Goris and Pieter and Cecelia in Amsterdam. We thank thee for the story. We thank thee for the Church of two or three gathered, for the assurance that whosoever loseth his life for thy sake and the Gospel's the same shall find it hereafter in eternal. And let us not fear men, which must perish like grass; but let us fear God, whose story shall abide forever." She thanks God for the story of the Anabaptists, a story of persecution and martyrdom. This is the spirit of Jesus.

Cecelia stood directly behind Goris and Pieter, holding her right hand over their heads: "Herewith I commend you to the Lord, and to the story of his grace. May He comfort, strengthen, stablish, you all with his Spirit, that you may finish that whereunto you are called, to the praise and glory of the Lord, so that we may rejoice together, and sit down at the Lord's table, where He shall serve us with new wine, in the kingdom of God, His father."[2] That is the spirit of Jesus.

The spirit of Jesus' people toward persecution is one of submission, thanksgiving, and gratitude, and this is what people schooled in the ways of the majority can't comprehend. What if Christianity wasn't meant to be

---

2. Campbell, *Cecelia's Sin*, 80.

a majority movement? We started out as a persecuted minority considered a cult. We were illegal in the empire. They hung us on crosses and then burned our bodies. By these standards we seem to have rejected Jesus and replaced him with a successful enterprise known as the church. Not wanting to face that belief in Jesus is a matter of life and death we prefer to think it a matter of no great consequence, as Flannery O'Connor said. One of her characters, honest enough to admit that he can't make peace with Jesus tries to violently reject him. He cries, "I preach the Church without Christ. I'm a member and preacher to that church where the blind don't see and the lame don't walk and what's dead stays that way."[3] We, being more sophisticated and subtle, have found more acceptable ways to push Jesus to the fringes of our lives.

The New Testament was written by a minority voice—a people on the run and under the gun but we read it as the majority faith of the most powerful nation in the world and the power of this world has gone to our head. The spirit of Jesus moves in the shadows from tree to tree, a wild ragged figure motioning to us to turn around into the dark where we are not sure of our footing, where we might be walking on water and not know it. Jesus searches high and low for those willing to find power in weakness and wisdom in folly. No wonder we have trouble reading the New Testament. We can't see the speck in the eyes of others because there is a log of majority privilege and authority stuck in ours.

I summon the voice of Cecelia once more to point us in the way that we should go: "Our Netherlands is no worse than the others. The lowering of the clouds of despotism and superstition hang dark over all of Europe today. Scenes of violence, of bloodshed, and oppression are rampant everywhere. That's the story we have written. But a land which gave us an Erasmus will one day grant us liberty. And when that meridian splendor makes its rounds it will light the way for all the world. Whatever the private interests of the princes, one day they will be a rare occurrence, and the fear they engender will be no more. A people who could snatch this ground from the sea will not let it be ruled forever by tyranny and falsehood. The blood of some may be in vain, but the red blood of Holland's martyrs will paint the corners of the earth. I would die for my Lord anywhere, but I am happy that He will let me die in Amsterdam."[4]

---

3. O'Connor, *Wise Blood*, 101.
4. Will Campbell, *Cecelia's Sin*.

Response

Are American Christians Persecuted?

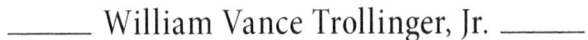 William Vance Trollinger, Jr. _____

IN THE UNITED STATES, Bible verses dot the billboard landscape. "In God We Trust" is on our coins, and politicians fall all over themselves to insert "God Bless America" in even the most mundane public addresses. 40–45% of Americans insist that they attended church the previous Sunday; that perhaps half of these folks are not telling the truth suggests the "social capital" that apparently accrues to churchgoing. Most important, perhaps, the Christian Right is the single most important constituency in one of the nation's two major political parties, and as the campaign for the 2016 Republican presidential nomination continues its frenzied and crazy course all of the candidates find themselves genuflecting to the Evangelical powers-that-be (and as one side effect, not one of these candidates will affirm that they believe in evolution).

On the face of it, then, the question "Are American Christians Persecuted?" is ludicrous. And yet, Dr. Kennedy is absolutely right to address this question in his sermon. A very large number of evangelicals and a good number of mainline Protestants and Catholics have been persuaded that laws and policies that reflect America's religious pluralism and that are designed to protect religious minorities are actually aimed to restrict the "religious freedom" of Christians. They have been convinced that there really is a governmental and cultural "War on Christmas" (a charge that, interestingly, first surfaced in the early 1920s, when the rabidly anti-Semitic

Henry Ford proclaimed that Jews had conspired to remove references to Jesus from Christmas cards). They have even been frightened into believing that—as the Creation Museum's Ken Ham claims—the day is near when we will see "the outlawing of Christianity" in America.

In response to this ideologically-driven nonsense Kennedy bluntly and rightly asserts that "spoiled, pampered, soft American Christians growling about their rights" know nothing of what it means to be truly persecuted. Christians in the US may on occasion be criticized on the grounds of their faith commitments; they may feel disdain from secular elites who associate Christianity with ignorance; they may have a sense of unease over the fact that Christian cultural hegemony is fading. But none of this constitutes persecution. In a brilliant and humorous rhetorical move that both clinches the case and invites congregants to hear what he is saying, Kennedy includes himself and his fellow preachers in the category of the soft and pampered, pointing out that "we have housing allowances, tax exemptions, and invitations to all the right social events, especially if a prayer is needed."

In short, and despite the confines of a 20-minute sermon, Kennedy dismantles the false narrative that American Christians are enduring persecution. Persuading Christians who have enjoyed and still enjoy "majority privileges" in the United States that they are not "victims" is important work. But what gives Kennedy's sermon real power is that, in his reference to John the Baptist and the 16th-century Anabaptists and the twenty-eight nations where Christians are persecuted today, he suggests the possibility that authentic Christianity will never be a "majority" religion, that authentic Christianity exists on the margins and in the shadows. That is to say, to truly follow Jesus is to invite persecution, as the Jesus message is always at odds with the powers-that-be.

This is important Gospel work, and in its emphasis on rejecting violence and loving one's enemies, it is certainly at odds with the culture, both American culture and much of American Christian culture. More than this, and again in the confines of a 20-minute sermon, he presents his case directly and powerfully. This said, this sermon—and here comes special pleading from the historian—could have been even stronger if Kennedy had done even more to root it in the history of the church. He points out that early Christians were "a people on the run and under the gun," but this point could have made much more vivid with reference to early Christian martyrs; for example, to include specific reference to the 3rd-century imprisonment and killing of Perpetua and Felicity in north Africa—a story so powerful that it was read annually in churches of the region—would confront 21st-century Americans with two women (one noble, one a slave) who refused to renounce their Christian faith and instead peacefully, even joyfully, accepted their violent deaths. While Kennedy makes good use of Will Campbell's novella, *Cecilia's Sin*, which provides a compelling account of Anabaptists preparing for martyrdom, the historical account of the 1527 trial, torture, and burning of Michael Sattler (followed by the drowning of his wife, Margaretha) could provide an even more powerful example as to what happens when Christians refuse to endorse the state's use of violence and who, as the memorial plaque at the execution site states, died in behalf of "the peaceful message of the Sermon on the Mount." And given the recent anti-Muslim hysteria in the United States, there would be real power in relating the story of the French Trappist monks in Algeria (dramatized in the film "Of Gods and Men") who were killed in 1996 by Islamic militants (or, the Algerian army) because they refused to leave Algeria and thus abandon their Muslim neighbors.

Given how poorly-versed American Christians are in church history, I cannot help but wonder if historical examples of persecution and martyrdom might make even more compelling the call to serve as witnesses to Jesus' work on the Cross. The stories of Perpetua and Felicity, Michael and Margaretha Sattler, and the Trappist monks in Algeria (and many, many more like them) corroborate Kennedy's remarkable statement near the end of this powerful sermon, that "the spirit of Jesus' people toward persecution is one of submission, thanksgiving, and gratitude, and this is what people schooled in the ways of the majority can't comprehend." Amen, and amen.

Response
Are American Christians Persecuted?

 Susan Trollinger

"America is a Christian nation."
"America is God's chosen nation."
"America is the greatest country on Earth."
"In America, anyone can succeed if they work hard enough."

For many Christians in the United States, these statements are true and uncontestable. There is no need to defend them. No evidence is required to substantiate them. Taken as truth, they serve as the basis for other claims such as that children should pray in public schools, that the US military should force other nations to adopt the US as their model for economy and/or government, and that anti-poverty programs are not just a waste of tax-payer money but are immoral. Dr. Kennedy adds to this list the following claim: "In the US, Christians are persecuted."

Like the claims listed above, the claim that Christians are persecuted in the US serves as the ground for other arguments. Chief among them is the argument that secular-liberal-humanists are winning a culture war that has undermined all that is good, right, and true in America and that it is time for all who call themselves Christian to stand up and fight to take back this country and restore it to its glory as the City on a Hill. Arguments like these matter because they effectively convince earnest Christians to brook no compromise. Whatever the issue—health care, the debt ceiling, immigration—good Christians must never waver on the truths they know since the character and future of this nation are at stake.

Today, we call these truths "truisms." Way back in the Fifth Century, BCE, in Athens when Western democracy was in early bloom, the Sophists (renowned for their ability to teach the art of persuasion, or rhetoric, in a city whose business was increasingly decided by arguments and speeches) called such truisms *doxa*.

The Sophists' notion of doxa was powerful for the way it enabled Athenians to think about truth in a new way. For people who grew up in, say, Athens or some other ancient Greek city-state, the truths of that city-state about what it meant to be Greek, what sort of government was best, who was their true enemy, and so forth seemed true and uncontestable. But for Sophists who taught rhetoric across city-states, "truths" that were indisputable in one city-state often differed significantly from the "truths" of other city-states. Thus, in Sparta the truth about a free woman was that she was educated, athletic, and visible in public; in Athens, she had no need for formal education, ought to marry very young, and must be kept inside the home.

For the Sophists, noticing that "truth" differed from one city-state to another was important because it suggested that what seems beyond doubt isn't. The Sophists knew that the way Athenians thought about free women was not the only way to think about them. Maybe the Athenians had "woman" right; maybe the Spartans did. Or maybe they both had it wrong.

From this insight, the Sophists inferred that on any question there is never just one answer. Moreover, they taught that the job of the rhetorician is to enable the audience to see that this is so. Thus, the Sophists regularly spoke about the most seemingly irrefutable truths. They challenged them, offered up alternative truths, and then invited their audiences to decide what the truth really was. What the Sophists provide today, then, is the idea rhetoric done well has the power to undermine the presumption of "truths" that may not be true at all. They also teach us that good rhetoric empowers people to think for themselves.

While many preachers in the US build mega-churches by massaging such popular truths as the following: that America is God's favored nation, that extending a hand to the poor just makes them dependent, that all liberals are relativists, and so forth, Dr. Kennedy (with a PhD in rhetoric) takes a different tack. Taking a page out of the Sophists' playbook, Kennedy cannot rest easy in the comfortable doxa of the day. Instead, he turns it on its head and invites us to think for ourselves.

Christians in America are not persecuted, he argues. On the contrary, they are favored in all sorts of ways. Moreover, he continues, whereas Christians in the past knew that preaching/living the Gospel could mean persecution in the form of real bodily, Christians today cringe at the thought of "speak[ing] of Jesus in public" for fear of appearing stupid or weird.

Kennedy, the Sophist, serves us well by overturning the popular truths that both mask our privilege as Christians in America and embolden us, thanks to larger arguments about the culture war, to show no mercy to those who are, in fact, persecuted—the poor, the immigrant, the other.

But there is more. Not satisfied (like the Sophists) to turn truth on its head so that we can think for ourselves, he pushes the good purpose of rhetoric further. Whereas the Sophists seemed content to promote a politics that seeks to enable people to think for themselves, Kennedy puts rhetoric in the service of a politics of Jesus. For Kennedy, it is not enough to turn the worldly-Christian truths on their heads. He wants to show us that if we mean to follow Jesus, we better focus our eyes on the Cross to be a people, not of God's favor or of world domination, of "submission, thanksgiving, and gratitude."

Having turned the "American-Christians-are-persecuted" truth on its head, Kennedy the *Christian* Sophist turns that truth again, this time not so as merely to negate it but, instead, in order to remind us that Christians *should* be persecuted. Or, better put, that Christians should preach/live the Gospel so boldly that the powers would find it necessary to persecute us. Rather than pine after the status of God's chosen nation, he implores Christians, we ought to follow Jesus on the Cross and become a people who "find[s] power in weakness and wisdom in folly."

Of course, if you want to win a culture war, "submission, thanksgiving, and gratitude" probably won't be your weapons of choice. Identifying the enemy, demonizing it, and cooking up strategies to destroy it (or at least kick it out of the US) are likely to seem much more effective. And that may be so, if it's a war you want to fight. But Jesus wasn't a warrior. He didn't seek victory in a culture war or any other. For those who wanted the Messiah to be a warrior-king, Jesus was a disappointment, dying in the most humiliating fashion in the face of his enemies.

"American Christians are persecuted." Jesus would surely find such a claim laughable. "To be good Christians, we need to fight a war against secular liberals, immigrants, the poor, Muslims." Jesus would surely find that claim laughable too. But living as we do in a culture of fear, anxiety, and competition, it's hard for us to get the joke.

Thankfully, we have Christian-Sophists, like Dr. Kennedy, who (because they have studied the Bible long and hard and have consulted the wisdom of the ages) know which truths of the Bible are "load-bearing" and can show us the folly of our worldly "truths" and the wisdom of the Lamb.

11

Jesus and ISIS

*2 Samuel 7:1–16, Ephesians 2:11–22,
Gospel Lesson: Mark 6:30–34, 53–56*

YES, I AM GOING to talk about JESUS and ISIS, but there's some intellectual undergrowth that needs to be cleared away. Even Christians probably wonder what Jesus can do about ISIS? How should the pulpit respond to current events?

Any attempt to engage in controversial current events from a pulpit entails serious risk. That, of course, should not be an obstacle for preachers.

There's a particular nasty weed that grows in our theological garden. It's a litany, a chorus, an unwritten rule. Its roots are so deep that you expect book, chapter, and verse citation after saying it: Never talk about politics, sex, and money." Some of you have often told me that you prefer to never talk about any current event. This feeling has extraordinary power in the church.

Walter Brueggemann, in *Truth Speaks to Power: The Countercultural Nature of Scripture* shows how we often embrace the established truth of the status quo, the conventional wisdom of the culture and then automatically assume this is the Christian response. Michel Foucault has shown us in graphic language how the cords of truth and power are entangled. Brueggemann then says, "Thus the Bible itself is a sustained contestation over truth in which conventional modes of power do not always prevail"[1] We do this

---

1. Brugeggemann, *Truth Speaks to Power*, 6.

almost automatically in America. We speak American, and we kind of fit the Christian into that. The question is how can we learn to speak as Christians in a manner that our language is not overtaken by the presumption that Christianity is not about sustaining the freedom of the individual? In fact, Christianity is not at all about sustaining the freedom of the individual. It's about the triumph of the Son of God through the cross and the resurrection. It is hard for us to grasp that there is a truth that is not American, not part of the establishment, not part of what almost everyone with good sense believes.

Since we often try to read the Scripture innocently, we miss Jesus saying, "You have heard it said" (there's the conventional wisdom, the cultural truth, the truth of the establishment), but I say to you (and there's the counter truth, the truth of Jesus). How do we miss this? It never crosses our mind that Jesus' blistering condemnation of Pharisees and scribes may be addressed to us rather than others. We can't read Scripture innocently no matter how deeply you may desire a literal truth. Literal truth reduces the truth, makes the truth an ideology, a form of idolatry. Literal truth imprisons the counter truth that is stated ironically, metaphorically.

The church always has to decide whether to be the mouthpiece of the establishment (hand-tamed by the gentry) or the risky alternative truth. My entire ministry has been a weird dance around the mantra—"Talk about anything in the world, anything at all, but don't talk about politics, sex, and money." Let me try to explain why I am so determined to undermine this particular noxious bromide. I appreciate this inclination to not create tension, but it overlooks the fact that the tension is already there. Without tension, without contested truth claims, we can't grow. We must choose between "I just want everyone to get along" and "I want a word from the Lord."

A church where everyone is expected to agree has sacrificed its mind to the gods of appeasement. Winston Churchill said, "An appeaser is one who feeds a crocodile, hoping it will eat him last." Maybe you are thinking, "But aren't we supposed to get along with one another and love one another?" Of course, but this overlooks the context of division and strife and arguments and ill-treatment in the church. You can't read I Corinthians 13 without reading I Corinthians 1. Paul writes, "It has been reported to me by Chloe's people that there are quarrels among you." Chloe had people? Apollos had people? Peter had people? After dealing with an array of sexual, financial, and political issues, Paul finally says, "Love is the greatest of the gifts."

After last Sunday's sermon on persecution, I received an email from Everett. He gave me permission to share the email: "Rod, I was thinking of Christian persecution for a few days before your sermon, not of American Christians but of those in the Middle East being driven out of their homes and homeland in majority Muslim countries. Can you give us a sermon on this? Arab Christians, our brothers and sisters in Christ, are being murdered in the Middle East. American Christians are mostly ignoring their plight. Conservative evangelical Christians are obsessed with their support of Israel and belief in the Rapture. Left-wing preachers are afraid to be critical of the Middle East policy of President Obama. And those ancient churches of the Middle East (Eastern Orthodox, Chaldean, Maronites, Copt, Assyrian) seem weird to many American Catholics and evangelicals.

Iraq's Catholic Chaldean Patriarch Louis Sako spoke searing words: "We feel forgotten and isolated. We sometimes wonder, if they kill us all, what would be the reaction of Christians in the West?" Pope Francis calls it a third world war, a form of genocide. At a summit convened in Damascus, the heads of five major eastern Christian churches of Antioch said the ideological well springs of hardline Islamism must be dried up by teaching, "a culture of openness, peace and freedom of belief."

We must speak for them. We must stand up for them. We must apply pressure to President Obama to take action. We must find ways to provide humanitarian aid. Why aren't UN troops protecting these Christians? Why aren't we agitating for somebody to go get our brothers and sisters and save them? In the Old Testament reading today we discover that God wouldn't let David build the temple because David had blood on his hands. What we have to offer is our witness, the power of our non-violent practices, and the gospel of Jesus. There are two competing truths in the narrative: one celebrates David as a mighty warrior and one sees David's violence as a violation of covenant. And it came to pass as they came, when David was returned from the slaughter of the Philistine, that the women came out of all cities of Israel, singing and dancing, to meet king Saul, with tabrets, with joy, and with instruments of music. And the women answered one another as they played, and said, Saul hath slain his thousands, and David his ten thousands.

And the contested truth: David has violated the covenant of holiness and has blood on his hands. We have to catch our breath and stand very still for a moment as we confront the truth about our own involvement in stories of violence. I think this is our story. We too have contested truth claims. We are embedded in war and violence. Born out of war, our history littered with wars piled on wars, and yet a nation with all kinds of Christian connections. This is our story and we should always be willing to live in the tension. We are violent Christians. There's still a lot of Andrew Jackson in the American spirit.

In today's reading from Ephesians we read: "For [Jesus] is our peace; in his flesh he has made both groups into one and has broken down the dividing wall, that is, the hostility between us." (Ephesians 2:14). This is our message but I fear we have forgotten how powerful it is. "Blessed are the peacemakers" is not intended as a theological bromide but as actual Christian practice. When enough people, of all nations, offer peace and an unrelenting message of condemnation of the violence of ISIS, change will come. It is up to us to give peace a chance by living nonviolent lives. Be vulnerable and open to making relationships with people different from us. We are afraid that this won't work because we are so enmeshed in violent ways.
Vulnerability is a relational term. There's no personal relationship with a belief or a text of the Bible. It takes other people to make relationships. All our fighting over beliefs and doctrines and issues indicates that we are not very good at forging relationships with one another. Being Christian is not signing off on a set of propositions — but is rather being embedded in a community of practices that make those beliefs themselves work and give us a community by which we are shaped. Faith is a speech act—"a performance just like you'd perform *Lear*. When Christians make everything about right beliefs and right stances on social issues there is a hardness that develops, an estrangement in the heart from those who refuse to go along. When the only thing at stake is a text the potential for argument, disagreement, mistrust, and hatred grows. This is how zealots end up justifying the murder of those who read texts differently. There's no relationship.

How can we know how to respond to Muslims when we don't even know a single Muslim? Have you ever prayed with a Muslim? Have you had dinner with a Muslim? Do you have any Muslim friends? Have you read the Koran? Have you knowledge of Ramadan? Have you ever attended a Muslim worship service?

After 9/11 we became a fearful people and we are going to make the world pay for scaring us to death. After all, we are not really convinced that Jesus is more powerful than ISIS. We believe, against all Christian teaching to the otherwise, that Jesus can't help us with terrorism and violence. When US Marines are being gunned down in Chattanooga, Tennessee it is hard to believe that we can trust in Jesus to do anything at all to help us. "As he went ashore, he saw a great crowd; and he had compassion for them, because they were like sheep without a shepherd; and he began to teach them many things. And wherever he went, into villages or cities or farms, they laid the sick in the market-places, and begged him that they might touch even the fringe of his cloak; and all who touched it were healed."

If the Christian response is not violence, how in the world can we expect to make a difference? I am appealing for a powerful Christian witness that refutes every act of oppression, abuse, prejudice, terrorism in our world. I am asking for the peace of Christ. I am asking for the most powerful worship in the world. If we faithfully participate in the liturgy that's called Word and Table; that's all we need. Here's the deal: we gather every Sunday to refuse the powers and principalities in the Sacrament of Holy Communion as the body of Christ and we go forth in the power of the Holy Spirit renewed and holy. Worship is designed to keep our souls from shriveling.

The bad seed of our hyper-individualism, our refusal to embrace world-wide neighborliness, is coming home to roost in America. We have a new brand of terrorism—isolated, frustrated, alienated young men. The CIA, the FBC, the entire alphabet of security agencies can't see any of these young men coming. They buy the illusion of violence and they act alone and they kill innocent people. Charleston, South Carolina—white supremacist. Chattanooga, Tennessee—Muslim with no apparent ties to radical groups. The Boston Marathon bombers. The Colorado cinema killer. The Army base murderer. The killing of unarmed African Americans. And the more frightened we become the more repressive we become. We are going to make the world pay for scaring us to death and we have the power to do it. NRA obsession with guns will be an afterthought if we ever unleash our real arsenal. American fear may lead to nuclear holocaust.

Our problem is that Christianity has been made easy. Our faith and way of life is being contested by religious expressions where adherents maintain maximum spiritual zeal, make any sacrifice, go any distance, and evangelize non-stop and we are easy-going, spoiled, pampered, hit-or-miss, take-it-or-leave it minimum commitment people. Religious zealots are soldiers in training; we are like tourists on a sight-seeing tour. Religious zealots are at war; we are at cocktail parties.

There is a historical precedent for this compromise of vibrant faith for a place in the culture. In the first century the Jews made a deal with the

Romans: political loyalty to Rome in exchange for not being too missionary and open with their faith. The church has made the same deal with American culture. In return for allowing us to participate fully in the benefits, status, and power of the culture, we implicitly agreed that we would keep our faith locked up in the church. This is a guerrilla war and we think it's a tea party. America needs more prophetic preachers, fewer politicians.

Around the world, the Muslim faith is growing because is not easy to be a faithful Muslim. They are more intense, more evangelical than we are, and less distracted by the secular culture that is enmeshed in our churches. A people who pray five times a day are probably racking up a lot more prayer miles than most Christians who may not even be members of the frequent prayer club.

What we have to offer is our witness, the power of our non-violent practices, and the gospel of Jesus. This is hard because we just don't have the time to fit in all this Christian training, practice, and performance in our busy schedules. Our children need to know the stories of Jesus, but this is complicated by how hard it is for young parents to get to church on Sunday for three or so hours. One of the vital tasks we have is to teach our children the stories of Jesus. We are doing that here at FBC. It happens every Sunday morning when Barbara Bogan and others teach our children the stories of Jesus. Think of our Sunday school teachers as terrorist fighters.

The teaching of violence as a philosophy always precedes violence as a practice. You must be taught to hate but you can also be taught to love and live in peace. Let's make sure that we have in place best practices for educating our children in the ways of peace. It is time for a more inclusive interfaith, interracial association of peacemakers. The bitter sectarians have failed us and must step aside to give peace a chance. It is time for a peace table that stretches from D. C to Damascus. It is time to give our grandchildren a peaceful world. Out with the warmongers; in with the peacemakers. The peace table's time has come. But we have far to go. Christians who love peace, who preach peace, who live peaceful lives, must reach across all the barriers to clasp hands with Muslims who love peace, Hindus who love peace, Jews who love peace, Buddhists who love peace, all peoples of all faiths. Get the peace-loving , marijuana-smoking Rastafarians to the table. Get all the people who despise all forms of oppression, terrorism, hatred, and exclusion and turn that into a mighty movement for peace. It is time for a movement by the people of faith that is outside the political parties.

It is time to stop going hat in hand to the politicians and speak the prophetic truth to power.[2] Preachers have no business being afraid of the powers. After all, we stand in the tradition of the prophets who spoke truth to power. Moses, Elijah, Nathan, Amos, John the Baptist, and Jesus. The powers would be shocked. "Now Elijah the Tishbite said to Ahab." Nobody saw that coming. Elijah didn't even have an appointment. It would be like Rodney the Redneck said to President Obama. The White House staff would be in a tizzy. We never heard of this fellow. We don't know how he got in here. We have no idea why he claims to have received a word from the Lord. He didn't even go to a good school. "This is the word of the Lord to President Obama: Not by might, nor by power, but by my spirit, says the Lord of hosts. We may pontificate about nuclear treaties with Iran and beat the drums for war, but it's just more politics as usual. The president proposes; the other side opposes. It's all so boring. I am no longer convinced that our politicians care about America, care about our future. They care about getting elected. They think the center of power is in the White House and the truth says the center of power is in the house of God. That puts us in grave danger because Americans are no longer going to the house of God and think it is irrelevant. But when the house of God falls, the nation falls. It happened once at Shiloh. The whole thing fell down. The old priest, Eli, fell and broke his neck and his sons were killed and a baby was named Ichabod—the glory of God has departed. It happened to Israel and it happened to Judah. And the house of God became a den of thieves. The truth dismisses politicians from center stage. Politicians need prophets. Where would Lincoln have been without the prophetic influence of the Quakers? Where would Johnson have been without Martin Luther King, Jr? Where is a prophet when we need one so desperately?

I'm weary of the buttoned-down orchestrated façade of American politics with its posturing, its hypocrisy, its lust for money. America, like Israel, needs to be looking for Elijah to come—that inexplicable, inscrutable agent loosed in history, subject to none of the conventional forms of power and accountable only to God. Finally shall come the one who has no tools of authority but "Thus says the Lord." The politicians always learn toolate that their power is useless. Remember Saul, his kingdom finished, his crown worthless, at the feet of the witch of Endor, conjuring up the

---

2. Preachers have no business being afraid of the power. After all, we stand in the tradition of the prophets who spoke truth to power: Moses to Pharaoh, Elijah to Jezebel, Nathan to David, Amos to Jeroboam, John the Baptist to Herod, and Jesus to Pilate.

ghost of Samuel. He knew too late that he needed a prophet. Without a prophet we are going to lose our moral consciousness and everything, everything will be for sale—from the penthouse to the White House. Maybe that's the attraction of Donald Trump—he's a real estate magnet; he can move the property.

Where are the prophets in Islam? Judaism? Christianity? Has God raised up Pope Francis as more prophet than pope? I'm pulling for him. The goodness in Christianity is going to have to merge with the goodness in Islam and Judaism to beat back the rising tide of violence and terrorism that only end badly for the world. Dr. King said, "We can no longer afford to worship the God of hate or bow before the altar of violence. The oceans of history are made turbulent by the ever-rising tides of hate. History is cluttered with the wreckage of nations and individuals that pursued this self-defeating path of violence."[3] It is our task to make peace more interesting than war. The age for peacemaking has come. Will you join?

---

3. King, Jr. Nobel Peace Prize acceptance speech, December 10, 1964.

Response
Jesus and Isis

———— Kyle Childress ————

IN ONE OF THE footnotes to this sermon, Rodney Kennedy says, "Risk is the middle name of a person called to preach the Gospel." If that's true, and I think it is, Rodney's middle name is risk. And after reading this sermon, it might be his first name, too.

First, the sermon title is risky, even provocative. Part of the danger in such titles is that at first glance it looks as if Rodney is indulging in some topical preaching and picking and choosing his own subject matter and texts. It is true; on occasion preachers need to depart from the lectionary to preach on some pressing issue, perhaps within the congregation or something in their local community, or perhaps a crisis in the wider world, which is what "Jesus and Isis" looks like. But Rodney does not do that. These are the lectionary texts appointed for the eighth Sunday after Pentecost year C. Rodney doesn't pick them; he just preaches them, which is one of the reasons this sermon has punch and potency. It arises from the given texts and therefore is clear that this is the Gospel speaking to this particular congregation rather than a sermon based upon the whims of the preacher.

At the same time, this sermon is particular; it speaks to this specific congregation. Readers of this sermon have a sense that we are overhearing an ongoing conversation between the Gospel, the pastor, and the congregation in their real-life context. It is not abstract; it is incarnational with specific names of congregation members mentioned, and the arguments put forth by Rodney sound to the reader like we are walking midway into a lively conversation. And it is lively: there is a kinetic quality to this sermon; it pops and moves, and even on the printed page we readers pick up some of the vitality and energy. Rodney writes for the ear, not for the eye, and the reader can "hear" the sermon as she or he reads it.

But these same qualities point to some of the challenges in this sermon. It moves all over the place. Never dull—and Lord God, save us from dull sermons about a Gospel that is life-changing and world-transforming—but it moves from theological and philosophical "undergrowth" (Rodney's term in the first sentence) into a kind of argument with his congregation about why provocative preaching should be part of a good, healthy, Gospel centered, arguing-it-out-church. Disagreements are part and parcel of who a church is and what a church is to be about, and as I've said, we readers feel like we're overhearing this ongoing argument, yet the downside is that we get close to becoming impatient with it. After awhile we want to say, "Okay, already. Get to the text and the core of the sermon!" It's not until a quarter of the way into the sermon when citing the email exchange with a church member asking for a sermon about the current refugee and immigration crisis in the Middle East that we say "Ah, now we're getting to what this sermon is going to be about." And it's not for another page that we finally get to one of the Scripture texts for the day.

I recall that Frederick Buechner once referred to Dostoevsky's *The Brothers Karamazov* as a great sprawling "bouillabaisse" of a novel. The image comes to mind in reading this sermon. It seeks to speak to the big issues of the day with the large word of the Gospel—none of that "three ways to be a happy family" kind of sermon—and it has everything in it: reflections on how congregations should argue and how they should interpret the Bible, how the Gospel of Jesus Christ calls us to fight evil, how the American church deals with the Middle East, how we deal with refugees and immigrants, the performative nature of Scripture and of the Christian life, Fundamentalism, the call to the Word and Table, prayer, Sunday School and children, books for further reading, and on and on. This large sermon sort of washes over a congregation; there is almost too much to take in at one sitting. Each one of these "issues" begs for a full sermon by itself. One of the great things about being a pastor is that there is always next Sunday and another sermon; not everything needs to loaded into one sermon.

This bouillabaisse of a sermon contains some wonderfully tasty and spicy morsels, phrases and images that give the readers and hearers succinct and thought-provoking insights. When comparing the rigors of Muslim practice with the weakness of much of American Christianity, Rodney says, "A people who pray five times a day are probably racking up a lot more prayer miles than most Christians who may not even be members of the frequent prayer club." It's a fun and quick image that is likely to be ruminated upon during the drive home from church. Or when contrasting the Gospel of Peace with the disciplined training terrorists undergo, Rodney says, "Sunday school teachers are terrorist fighters" as he reminds his congregation how important having children in Sunday morning Bible study is. "Violence is sensational but not permanent" is a powerfully memorable line from his discussion of the temptation to use violence to solve problems.

About halfway through the sermon Rodney quotes Stanley Hauerwas, "Faith is a speech act—'a performance just like you'd perform *Lear*...'" This sermon is a speech act. It does something. It overwhelms readers with the Good News of Jesus Christ; the peace, love, and hope of Jesus do not simply counter hate and violence but overcomes them. Furthermore, this sermon needs to be heard. And if Rodney preaches in person with the same gusto that comes across on the page, it is a performance I'd like to hear.

12

The Holy Spirit as Reading Teacher
Acts 15

Do you remember your first grade reading teacher? My first grade reading teacher was Inez Andrews. She seemed like a god to me. She was 22 and fresh out of college with a bachelor's degree in elementary education and a teaching certificate. Words fell from her lips like gold and my eager mind took in every syllable. I could never have guessed that Mrs. Andrews had opened the kingdom of knowledge to me and that I would be reading every day for the rest of my life. Like the novelist, Pat Conroy, "I never feared taking any unchaperoned walks through the fields of language. Words lifted me up and filled me with pleasure. I've never met a word I was afraid of. When reading a book, I'll encounter words that please me, goad me into action, make me want to sing a song."[1] Dick and Jane first grade primers were works of wisdom in her hands. Mrs. Andrews gave me the keys to the kingdom.

Well, we all have the most powerful reading teacher in the universe for our instruction. Meet the Holy Spirit. The Holy Spirit teaches us to read the Bible.[2] And the Holy Spirit is a provocative teacher. What's the point of a teacher that doesn't set our hearts aflame? The best teachers know what strings to pull to motivate a student. The Holy Spirit is the grandest

---

1. Conroy, *My Reading Life*, 86.
2. Fowl, *Engaging Scripture*, 97.

motivator of all. If you need motivating, ask the Holy Spirit for a pep talk. But be prepared. There's no telling what she will insist you do.

I pray that some of you may fall in love with Scripture all over again. Throughout this sermon I am promoting a holy and reverential respect for the study of the bible—the slow, difficult work of poring over sentences, phrases, and words to discern meaning. It is this kind of story that affirms the conviction of the faithful that these words of Scripture are truth-bearing. After all conservative Christians accuse us of not taking the Bible seriously as a guide for faith and life. I want to challenge this assumption. No Christian group has the copyright for the depository of biblical meaning. Conservative evangelical Christians have planted their flag in the soft calfskin leather of the Bible like astronauts claiming the moon as American property. Well, they are a bunch of claim jumpers. The claim is in dispute about the Bible.

I have learned that there is a pressure that comes from the Scripture, a pressure that is designed to lead to repentance (change of mind, change of heart). The pressure of the text on our lives is a good that exists for the unity and strength of the church. I have no interest in alleviating this pressure. After all, we do have a propensity to avoid what we know is good for us like a child refusing to eat any food that is green in color. If I knew that cucumbers were the healthiest, most nutritious food in the world and they would add years to my life, I would stop going around saying, "I don't like cucumbers" and I would eat cucumbers. "I don't like it" is just not a strong enough reason to give up church or Bible or God. For centuries the church has been saying, "This is good for you" and like three-year-olds the people have been whining, "But I don't like it." It has gotten so bad that even preachers now have planning retreats and marketing surveys and focus groups to find out what people like and how to provide for their satisfaction in Sunday worship. This puts a lot of pressure on me, because I want you to like me, but the claims of the gospel—the most pressure that can be applied to the human mind and heart—will not let me alone.

When is the last time you paused to take stock of how your Christian experience is doing in the cross-pressures of a secular culture? It is so easy to get thrown out of the orbit of conscious Christian discipline and into the outer space of secularity where there is no gravity, no grounding. You just float around and around at increasingly faster speeds attempting to dodge all the debris in the secular space. How many of us make decisions—from

THE HOLY SPIRIT AS READING TEACHER

the ordinary to the difficult—on the basis of common sense, experience, advice from friends and families, and instinct? And while you are spinning around at increasingly dangerous speeds that are hard on your heart and other vital organs, you build up a negative pressure known as stress and pieces of your spiritual immune system are ripped from you. Do you mind if I ask you to check and see if you are aligning your life with the movement of the Holy Spirit and the teaching of Scripture in your daily life?

There's a consistent pattern to the pressure that we can follow throughout Scripture. Jesus proposes; his church opposes.

Jesus advances; his church retreats.

Jesus offers the new; his church clings to the old.

Jesus breaks old barriers; his church rebuilds old walls.

There's a pattern.

Jesus commands; his church resists.

Jesus offers new wine; his church clutches to old bags.

Jesus crosses old boundaries; his church redraws the lines.

Jesus teaches us new ways; we reject.

Jesus says, "Embrace the new;" his church huddles with the old.

The Holy Spirit tells Peter to rise and eat and Simon protests. The Spirit tells Simon to go to the home of Cornelius and Peter is reluctant and puzzled by the meaning of the vision. The Holy Spirit tells Peter to testify about the gospel to Cornelius and Peter gives the worst testimony in the history of testifying: "You yourselves know that it is unlawful for a Jew to associate with or to visit a Gentile." Peter makes it clear that he is only at the home of Cornelius because the Holy Spirit made him do it.

Not everyone responds the same to pressure. Some fold like a scared poker toward illegal aliens and Muslims. It would be different if we thought along with the Holy Spirit. There's a pattern of outsiders modeling the faith of God's people. There's Rahab the Canaanite harlot the first to confess Israelite faith in the Promised Land. Rahab's name was probably an old soldiers' joke. The Semitic word means 'wide'; in Ugantic eipi literature it appears as a term for the female genitalia. People heard the name and chuckled; they knew what to make of this 'broad,' or so they thought"[3] We have lost the shock so let me update the story. God picks a Third Street prostitute to bear the good news and not a member of the respectable First Baptist Church. There's the Canaanite woman Jesus called a "dog," standing her ground begging for her child to be healed and Jesus says, "O woman, great

---

3. Davis, *The Art of Reading Scripture*, 173.

is your faith!" There's the Roman centurion pleading for his daughter's life and Jesus says he has not found faith like this in all of Israel. There's the one leper out of ten who came back and praised God and Jesus asks, "Was no one found to return and give praise to God except this foreigner?" And he said to him, "Rise and go your way; your faith has made you well." There's a pattern: outsiders act like insiders. Gandhi and nonviolence. Bill Gates and immunization of children in Africa and education in America. The Holy Spirit not only surprises; she shocks our religious sensibilities and all I can say, "You go, girl!"

The outsiders are doing God's will. So let your self-righteous shock, your measly piousity turn to surprise when the Holy Spirit swoops into the heart of the early church and invites the outsiders to become insiders. In Jesus there are no outsiders.

In our Acts reading the Holy Spirit makes moves that the church didn't anticipate and with which the majority disagreed. Gentiles are invited to join the church without circumcision, but the church resisted. The church said, "No, that's not how we do things around here." Spirit or no Spirit, these Christians insist that Gentiles can't be part of the church unless they are circumcised.

Where did they get this idea? Scripture that's where! "God said to Abraham, "[12]Throughout your generations every male among you shall be circumcised when he is eight days old[14]."[4] Timothy Luke Johnson says that we must appreciate the force of their position. It was theologically respectable. Scripture says it is a dangerous thing to fall into the hands of the living God. Well, I think it dangerous to fall in with a bunch of Christians running around claiming, "It's in the Bible. The Bible tells me so." There's no stubbornness like a people convinced they have the Bible on their side.[5] Some of the church's worst ideas originate in Scripture.

Now, I want you to think about this for a moment. How can you have Scripture on your side and be wrong? If all your life you have been taught by your parents, grandparents, pastors, teachers that you have the Bible on your side, no wonder you are up in arms when someone comes along and tells you there's a new reading.

---

4. Genesis 17:9–14, *NRSV*. 10

5. See Kathleen C. Boone, *The Bible Tells Them So*. See also *Engaging Scripture, Irony and Meaning in the Hebrew Bible, The Rhetoric of Fiction, How to Read the Bible, The Bible Made Impossible, Fundamentalism and Evangelicals, Apostles of Reason,* and *In Discordance with the Scriptures.*

THE HOLY SPIRIT AS READING TEACHER

The church faced with trouble right there in the Holy Land did what the church does: convene a conference. Have a denominational gathering and vote. The outcome is by no means certain. The conservative Christians are in the ascendancy. They have been in charge from the beginning. The twelve apostles were all Jewish Christians. But the Holy Spirit has picked off one of the apostles—the leader himself, Simon Peter. Even the Holy Spirit will show up with a ringer now and again.

Three spirit-filled leaders of the church—Peter, Paul, and Barnabas—speak in favor of including Gentiles without requiring circumcision. The Holy Spirit doesn't work with majorities but with a few willing persons. The Jerusalem Church voted to change the "plain sense" of Genesis 17:9–14 by recognizing the Spirit's work through the testimony of Peter, Paul, and Barnabas. James, the official leader of the conference, gives a wrap up speech and in it he says, "It seemed good to the Holy Spirit and to us"—Wow! Now, that's a positive approach to Scripture. Certainty has left the building. Proof is left without defense. Goodness rules! It seemed good to the Holy Spirit. I'm going to stick with that.

Response
The Holy Spirit as Reading Teacher

———— Jason Hentschel ————

A CENTURY AGO, A fellow Baptist preacher pressured by the gospel cried out: "If in our loyalty to the Church of the past we have distrusted thy living voice and have suffered thee to pass from our door unheard, we pray thee to forgive." In today's sermon, Rod Kennedy offers a similar confession. The gospel, he suggests, is more than simply the story of Jesus Christ crucified, dead, and buried. As the good news, it is a double-edged sword, splitting the bone and marrow of our most certain certainties. The gospel overturns false preconceptions and redirects misplaced and misfocused religiosity. It bears an intrinsic incisiveness, what Kennedy calls its "pressure that is designed to lead to repentance." From first-century circumcision to modern racism and a patriarchal pulpit, the church has a history of finding its dogmatism questioned, its interpretations upended.

The Book of Acts is full of shock and awe. It tells the story of God's act to extend his promise out beyond the chosen people. Here the Spirit reveals the "scandal of particularity" that is salvation through Jesus Christ to be a genuine "blessing of universality." Indeed, the actual scandal of Acts is not so much Christ's particularity but his universality. This is intended to be shocking, and as Kennedy reminds us, if we grow comfortable in our beliefs, we risk dulling the gospel's cutting edge. Why, we are led to ask, did Peter believe God had accepted the gentiles when hundreds of years of scriptural interpretation said otherwise? The Book of Acts tells us repeatedly—because the Spirit told him so.

To be sure, there is a certain ambiguity in Kennedy's sermon here. When I originally heard it, Kennedy's rejection of certainty in scriptural interpretation came coupled with an intense sense of anticipation. Nobody knew where the Spirit was going to blow next, but we did not feel paralyzed by uncertainty and instability. We felt enlivened by hope. Indeed, it seemed the Spirit had already set our hearts aflame. Here was a guide we could trust to heal the world, though we did not know what path she would take to get there. It would seem, however, that our anticipation and excitement that morning had the understandable effect of masking some of the sermon's ambiguity.

With all his talk about new readings and different interpretations and listening to the Spirit, Kennedy leads the proverbial elephant into the room, only to have us sit and stare at it. If the Spirit is both free to blow wherever she will, what then of the Bible? What then of God's past revelation given there? If the Spirit were truly our *reading* teacher, it would seem that *what* we read bears at least some importance for us. How then should we understand the relationship between the Spirit and the Bible? What actual *reading* help does the Spirit provide? Do we trust her to give that long lost—or, possibly, never had—definitive interpretation? If so, how is that any different from classical liberalism's attempt to get behind the text or literalism's parallel attempt to replace a dynamic God with a static book? Both try—unsuccessfully—to escape the contingencies of history and the contextual nature of interpretation itself. To be sure, Kennedy has elsewhere repeatedly argued against such moves. Should we then give him the benefit of the doubt and understand him to be claiming that the Spirit might teach by offering genuinely new revelation, new light for a new day and place? Whatever the case, the elephant looms.

Let us return to the biblical story. If we are being honest, the Book of Acts lives in a different world. Who among us receives visions like Peter? Who among us has been transported to far off places like Philip? Apart from having ecstatic visions ourselves, how then can we expect to distinguish between "it seemed good to the Holy Spirit" and "it seemed good to us"? How do we tell when that good is truly God's good? Do we not really only have "good *to us*"? Kennedy criticizes evangelicals for claiming to own the Bible, but their most desperate concern—a concern that has fueled their Bible battles for over a century now—is well made: How can we distinguish the voice of God amidst the sea of our own clamoring? Trusting the Holy Spirit as reading teacher is beautiful in theory, but what if we can't tell the Spirit apart from cousin Boudreaux and those very "cross-pressures of secular culture" scripture supposedly challenges?

To consider the decision of the Jerusalem council to be simply the apostles' discovery that scripture doesn't mean what they think it means is to stifle the gospel's radicalness. In Peter's rooftop vision and subsequent encounter with Cornelius, the Holy Spirit changes the rules of the game. While we might look back and see how all of this now makes sense, we dull the gospel's cutting edge by simply brushing off that old misinterpretation as the consequence of a lack of information. We have to remember that there are two conversions in Acts 10, and the focal one is not of Cornelius but of Peter. Indeed, in the flow of the story, the purpose of Cornelius' conversion is to support Peter's decision to turn away from the "party of the circumcised" and toward the new light of the gospel. This is the case not only in Acts 10, but in chapters 11 and 15 as well, where the story is repeatedly given in order to emphasize the radical, inclusive action of the Spirit. Kennedy notes that there was every scriptural reason to demand that gentiles be circumcised. Those earliest Jewish Christians had scripture on their side, and yet they were wrong. What changed their minds was an experience of the Spirit.

Back to that elephant. It would seem that Kennedy's point is best made if we do not view the Holy Spirit as someone who simply teaches us how to read and interpret a text correctly so that we can understand what it once meant and, on that account, what it means for all time. No, the Spirit actively reveals *herself* in our reading of scripture. And yet, as Curtis Freeman has put it, the trouble is that her voice is not always clear, and she has a habit of coming to us as some contesting "other." Let us then listen like those at the Jerusalem council who heeded the cutting edge of the gospel as it came riding on the voice of the Spirit—and then have the courage to say that it seems good to us as well.

13

Theology and Twitter!
Mark 6:6b–13

MARK TELLS US HOW Christianity started. Jesus sent out his twelve disciples in this radical itinerant ministry. He sent them into the villages and cities. They went without protection and without economic security. He gave them a message: Tell people to change the way they are living and enter the kingdom of God. This is our story and mission.

One question: What happened? Christians happened to the church. And look at us now. The church, by and large, has morphed into the proclaimer of the bad news. Some churches have become the big bad wolf, huffing and puffing and threatening to blow the house down.

Our culture is greatly reduced and rendered inane. And there is a symbol of how reduced and inane we are. Twitter! How many of you have a Twitter account? Well, I think Twitter symbolizes the emptiness of our culture. For example, I read that a harebrained Florida man has 270,000 Twitter followers. His hashtag is @_Florida-Man. Here are few nutty examples: "Florida man tries to walk out of store with chainsaw stuffed down his pants. Florida man falls asleep during sailboat burglary with gift bag on his head; can't be woken by police. Florida man accidentally shoots himself with stun gun while trying to rob the Radio Shack he also works at.[1] This is crazy talk but you know what's really crazy? 270,000 followers. By now, you should be asking, "But what does Twitter have to do with theology?"

---

1. Alvarez, "@_FloridaMan Beguiles With the Hapless and Harebrained."

Long before there was Twitter, Christians were "tweeting" half-truths in the form of slogans. A little Christianity is a dangerous thing. Tweet-like slogans have been with us from the beginning. There are biblical tweets—slogans used to prop up weak theology: Biblical slogans: The more I sin the more God's grace can be shown. Handle not. Touch not. Taste not. From libertines to legalists—slogans.

There are historical tweets: Cleanliness is next to godliness. No creed but the Bible. And a half-truth has more lives than a cat. The gospel is simple. God said it. I believe it. That settles it. It was God's will. All you have to do is love people and do your best. Everything happens for a reason. God helps those who help themselves. God won't give you more than you can handle. Love the sinner; hate the sin. Slogans end up being half-truths that are repeated until people believe them. Did you know that many people think that the sentence, "Cleanliness is next to godliness" is in the Bible? Its' a nice saying, but it is not in the Bible. As far as we know, John Wesley is the first person to ever say that cleanliness is next to godliness. Did you know that the claim that Baptists have no creed but the Bible wasn't spoken by a Baptist but by the founder of the movement that practically destroyed First Baptist Church—Alexander Campbell? Our 17th century forebears were not an anti-creedal people. It was a half-truth that continues to hamper our worship of God to this day. Did you know that the claim that Baptists don't like creeds because they were written by men and not in the language of the Bible is a half-truth? Of course the creeds were written by men; so was the Bible. And the language of the Apostles' Creed is thoroughly soaked in biblical grammar.

We get into trouble when we try to reduce complex arguments to a few words. One way this occurs is when we reduce the argument of a Christian scholar, preacher, or theologian to a few words and then interpret them differently than they were intended. For example, Martin Luther's famous phrase "sola Scriptura," has become a heresy in some ways. It becomes the seedbed of fundamentalism and biblical criticism in the academy divorced from the church. It assumes that the text of the Scripture makes sense separate from a Church that gives it sense. In the early centuries of the Church, most Christians were illiterate, but that did not in itself make them less faithful. That Christians have thought it possible to translate our Scriptures should be sign enough that no strong distinction can be made between text and interpretation. That Christians learned of Christ and Christ's relationship to Israel through biblical scenes portrayed on church windows and stone carvings and statues of the saints, alive and dead, should be sufficient for us to realize that the text of Scripture is not meant to be 'preserved intact' from the church. God certainly uses Scripture to call the Church to faithfulness, but such a call always comes in the form of some in the Church reminding others in the Church how to live as Christians—no "text" can be substituted for the people of God.

Let's unpack two of these half-truths and having heard them one last time never repeat them again.

The gospel is simple.

How odd that the most difficult, the most demanding faith in the world should be subjected by people to this half-truth. We should not be alarmed at the idea that Christianity requires a certain intellectual commitment from the disciples of Jesus Christ. I am not saying that the kingdom of God is for scholars only. I am challenging the half-truth that the gospel is simple, easy, and like saying the A, B, C's. The gospel is hard, but it is not simple.

In the book of James we are told, "Not many of you should become teachers. For all of us make many mistakes."[2] According to James, we are not capable of perfect interpretations of Scripture. We can't just read a verse off the page as it were and do what it says. What does this mean for those who claim the Bible is inerrant and infallible? We all make mistakes.. In order to have an inerrant Bible, written by God, you have to have inerrant readers and inerrant interpreters. There have never been any such people. The biblical authors were sinners; the readers of the Bible are sinners; the interpreters are sinners. If we are going to serve people as disciples of Jesus we must become trained spokespersons or teachers of the language of Christianity. No more saying the gospel is simple. If the gospel were simple we wouldn't be engaged in such a struggle over whether it is social or individual. Does that sound simple to you? "It is a fearful thing to fall into the hands of the living God."[3] Does that sound simple? "Work out your salvation with fear and trembling." Does that sound simple? "Hunger and

---

2. James 3:2, *NRSV*.
3. Hebrews 10:21, *NRSV*.

thirst for righteousness."[4] Take up your cross daily and follow Jesus. The gospel is not simple.

Our greatest sin is not that we do great wrong but rather than we are too adjusted and accommodated to the world as it is. Please stop telling people the gospel is simple. It is a bait and switch technique from 19th revivalism and it is time for it to go.

"God said it. I believe it. That settles it."

Some Christians like to desperately shout this slogan. Think about it. Do you really want to live by this half-truth? How odd that we pick out only a few texts and attach this slogan. There is too much historical evidence that the Bible has been read in ways that seemed to authorize appalling abuse, even murder, of women, Jews, slaves, colonized peoples, homosexuals. And God is right in the middle of it all. God authorized the destruction of entire villages and peoples. We can't actually read the Bible as if it appeared whole as a pure book with no historical and cultural influences. The Bible was written under the inspiration of the Holy Spirit but on the human side there was imperfection. In I Corinthians 7:25–26, Paul says, "Now concerning virgins, I have no command of the Lord, but I give my opinion as one who by the Lord's mercy is trustworthy." The Bible has pagan habits/cultural artifacts incorporated into its message. The most obvious one: slavery.

Still we live with its awful residue: racism. The God who says, "Behold I make all things new" cannot be nailed to the cross of Christian certainty in this awful slogan. "God said it. I believe it. That settles it," doesn't put you in charge of the universe or the truth.

Our delusion is that we are in charge. Steven Colbert was asked why he became a comedian. He said that the night his father and two of his brothers died in the crash of an Eastern airlines jet, he turned to humor out of disrespect for those who thought they were in charge of the world. I have a growing disrespect for preachers stomping around crying out that God said and we all have to fall in line and agree with what these preachers claim about God. As soon as a preacher goes apoplectic and claims God is going to destroy America he has become the religious equivalent of @_Florida-Man.

We don't have to be certain in order to speak for God. Barbara Brown Taylor argues that our language is broken by our denial of its uncertainty. "Sometimes I think we do all the talking because we are afraid won't. Or conversely, that God will." In a culture where you have to shout, keep it on

---

4. Matthew 5:6, *NRSV*.

a fourth grade level and make exaggerated claims, it is rare to find a space where people are willing to admit uncertainty and the struggle to express the truth about what it is to be human and hungry in a fallen world full of wonders" (*When God Is Silent*, 110).[5]

Instead of glib and cute we should be humble and hesitant in the face of what is mysterious and never fully known. The mystery overpowered Moses and he cried, "Lord, get someone else." See Isaiah on his knees: "I am a man of unclean lips."

Shouldn't those who speak for God now be reticent? Hesitant? Humble? Indirect instead of in-you-face? Yet sermons are filled with astounding statements: "God told me." "God spoke to me last night and told me to tell you." Every preacher should remember that just because we say so doesn't make it so.

Jesus tells us to seek, ask, knock, and search. Being trained in the truth is more like searching for buried treasure or a pearl of great price than selecting a stack of slogans from the Wal Mart of theology. "Sometimes it causes me to tremble" as I search for truth. Let St. Paul encourage us: "Do your best to present yourself to God as one approved by him, a worker who has no need to be ashamed, rightly explaining the word of truth."

---

5. Taylor, *When God Is Silent*, 110.

Response
Theology and Twitter

 Ethan Smith _____

"And those who belong to Christ Jesus have crucified the flesh with its passions and desires." Galatians 5:24

Dr. Kennedy's words have grown more salient since they were first proclaimed. A disturbing example of the problem he diagnosed in his sermon has reared its ugly head. The so-called simple truths of the Scriptures have recently been invoked by American Christians to excuse ourselves from the commands of Christ. In the wake of the terror attacks in Paris, many have insisted that the vulnerability involved in welcoming Christ-the-stranger in the figure of political refugees is too high of a risk to take. Although fear mongering and scapegoating aliens has been common in recent public discourse, we have recently witnessed a new found moral zeal in the refusal of hospitality to Muslims from Syria and Iraq.

In my experience, Twitter and Facebook have been alive with Scriptural justifications for Christian disobedience to the gospel. The most typical example is an absurd appeal to Romans 13: 1–7. The passage has been used as a divine command to governments to refuse any hospitality which might prove to be dangerous. The state is commissioned, according to the "plain sense" of the passage, to defend its people against those who would do them harm. It would, therefore, be disobeying its divine commission if it were to allow refugees into the U.S. who may turn out to be terrorists.

Leaving aside the failures of charity and accuracy in interpreting the moral relevance of these human beings solely in terms of "potential terrorism," why is this interpretation of Scripture absurd? Dietrich Bonhoeffer wrote the following about the text in question, St. Paul is talking to Christians, not the State. His concern is that the Christians should persevere in ... obedience ... whatever conflict should threaten them. He is not concerned to excuse or condemn any secular power. No State is entitled to read St. Paul's words a justification of its own existence ... His entire concern is with the responsibility of the Christian community towards the State.[1]

Against the apparent clarity of the text justifying the government's use of the sword, we should recall that this is the Letter to the Christians in *Rome*. The Roman government had recently tortured the Messiah to death and would soon make a martyr of Paul. Surely Paul does not mean to justify such actions.[2] Nor can Romans 13:1–7 be severed from the immediately preceding passage of 12:14–21 which commands hospitality, peace, and even love for one's enemies and those who persecute Christians (no doubt including the same government referred to in 13:1–7). Rather than anachronistically projecting modern distinctions of the individual and her religious responsibilities (Romans 12:14–21) and the government and its responsibilities (Romans 13:1–7) onto the text, we should locate the passage in its theological, historical, and literary context. In a political climate of fear and hostility, even when your mortal enemy bears the sword of the state, the commands of Jesus are binding.

It is precisely to historical and theological attentiveness in reading and preaching the Scriptures that Dr. Kennedy has called us, and to the humility that marks these disciplines. He has rightly argued that those who claim not to interpret Scripture, but merely believe what it "obviously" says, wish to make their own perspectives equivalent to God's. However, I want to ask why the problematic reading of Romans 13 can appear so persuasive?

The apparent "clarity" of Romans 13—or any number of Scriptural passages—is not a function of the text's character, but of readers' passions; of fear, pride, desire for vengeance, the lust for dominance, etc. Often times preachers point out that Satan tempted Christ by quoting Scripture, but fail to distance their own Scriptural interpretations from the "slavery" to

---

1. Bonhoeffer, *The Cost of Discipleship*, 262–63.
2. Recall that just prior his execution Jesus had caused a significant disturbance in the economic life of Roman occupied Israel by his riotous actions in the temple, proving he was a danger to many in power.

the "devil," "the fear of death (Hebrews 3:14–15)." The meaning of Romans 13:1–7 is obvious in a fearful world, especially when one believes her own interests to be protected by those in power. The passions' powers of distortion produce the desire for and illusions of Scriptural simplicity embodied in short, ego-centric "truths." Is it enough to counter the false-certainties produced by the passions to invoke the type of humility and hesitancy that Dr. Kennedy recommends?

It may be that Dr. Kennedy's gesture to an alternative falls short of the gospel's radical challenge to preach the gospel against the fear of death.[3] What is missing from the sermon is the hermeneutical Christo-centrism evinced by the Patristics.[4] There are many different ways in which Christo-centric hermeneutics are relevant to the problem at hand, but I will focus on asceticism. That is, only a prayerful Christological asceticism can read Scripture as over-against our distorted self-interests masquerading as morality which is itself the product of the "flesh's" powers to see and understand all things in light of the fear of death.

The Fathers had methods for dealing with seemingly problematic Scriptural texts and knew very well the depths of self-deception produced by the passion of fear. Maximus the Confessor wrote: "The cause of this deviation is the hidden fear of death."[5] The hiddenness of this fear refers to the fact that we are dealing with a phenomenon broader than mere episodic affect. Rather, "fear" names patterns of behaviors, habits, modes of attention, interpretations, etc. which are organized around the desire to avoid something real or imagined. The "hidden fear of death" names the many ways in which the avoidance of death organizes our lives on both conscious and unconscious levels. For the Fathers this included even the manner in which the basic desires of our "bodies of death" are prone to gluttony, lust, and aggression, and the manner in which thoughts and actions extend this inchoate fear. It is just these which constitutes the "worries" which Jesus said are the means by which the "Evil One" snatches away the word of the gospel sown in the heart (Matthew 13:10–23).

The difficulty is that this fear insinuates itself into our being at a level below our conscious minds and gives rise to many of our own thoughts. Ruminating on Christ's words, St. Macarius preached: To refrain from evil

---

3. It certainly fails to describe the fullness of the gospel challenge to the fear of death as embodied in most of Dr. Kennedy's own preaching.

4. And the Christo-centrism in most of Dr. Kennedy's sermons.

5. Maximus the Confessor, *Questions to Thalassius*, 61 (PG 90,633), 135.

is not perfection. Perfection is to enter into a spirit of humility and to put to death the serpent that is making its nest and practicing murder below even the spirit, deeper than the abode of thought, in the treasury and storehouse of the soul. For the heart is an abyss.[6]

We underestimate the depths from whence come our distortions of the Scriptures. The picture we should have of the fear of death taking control of one's thoughts and actions is not the paranoid who hoards survival gear and food or even those who drive themselves to obviously unconscionable acts because they have obsessively exaggerated the threat of others. Rather, we should picture the myriad of ways which we allow "responsibilities" to keep ourselves and our "group" safe to determine the meaning of the gospel.[7] We excuse ourselves from obligations the gospel places on us for figures such as the migrant, the criminal, those in "bad neighborhoods," the addicted, the enemy, etc. It is by interpreting such as these solely in the terms of the dangers they pose, seeing them through the lens of the fear of death, that we are snatched away from the word of the gospel sown in the heart.

The humility of which Macarius wrote is irreducibly Christo-centric and ascetic. Many of the Patristics did not shy away from acknowledging those Scriptural texts whose plain sense appear to call for reprehensible acts, and which could be and have been used to justify further evil acts. Rather than chalking these texts up to the culturally accepted evils of their human authors, theologians like Origen and Gregory of Nyssa insisted that the Spirit had placed these stories in Scripture as a means by which Christians are to develop the capacity to discern what is fittingly and unfittingly said of God, and so which such stories should or should not be read literally. Tales of God commanding ethnic cleansing, therefore, did not indicate an historical event but taught the extent and difficulty of the task of putting to death one's "flesh" and its passions and desires by which we want to believe in a God who commands such things be done to our enemies. The criterion for discerning what is fittingly said of God is always Jesus and the revelation of God in Christ. Furthermore, the true readings of these texts always referred to Christ and had to cohere with how he is presented in the Gospels.

The manner in which the Christo-centric hermeneutic is ascetic can be seen in light of an ancient monastic reading of one of the most disturbing passages in the Bible. Psalm 137:9 reads, "Happy shall they be who take

---

6. Pseudo-Macarius, *Eighteenth Homily* (PG 34, 633), 141.

7. These "responsibilities" are themselves typically founded on illusions of control.

your little ones and dash them against the rock!" To the monastics this text was figurative and referred to Christ.[8] The "little ones" are those inchoate thoughts which emerge into our conscious minds through the workings of the hidden fear of death. Such thoughts will always arise, and our capacity to resist entertaining them is not merely a matter of choice, but of training and struggle. The "rock" is the name of "Jesus" which the monk was to continuously invoke in rigorous and bodily prayer practices and return to whenever one's mind stubbornly insists on nourishing the "little ones" of fear, vengeance, lust, etc. with the food of attention. A life of resisting what our "passions and desires" tell us about God, the threat of others, our food, our safety, our pleasures and pains, etc. requires disciplines of joining our thoughts, our Scripture reading, our desires and their satisfactions, and more to that of Christ. In short, it requires the marriage of Christological hermeneutics with Christological asceticism.[9]

There is no space to satisfactorily develop what this asceticism entails, especially for those who are not monastics. Allow me to suggest, however, that living in an economic and political order which depends on inflaming the passions and desires we are called to crucify, it is unlikely we will uproot the sources of our self-serving uses of Scripture without intentional practices of disciplining and restraining these same passions and desires.

---

8. Clement, *Roots*, 171.

9. Evagrius Pontus, the great and influential teacher of ascetical struggle, argued that the anger expressed in the Psalms is only appropriately directed toward the demonic and one's own evil passions. In the light of Christ's teachings and example one could not use the Psalms any other way without lapsing into disobedience. See Bunge, *Despondency*, 27.

Bibliography

Agam-Segal, Reshef. "Contours and Barriers: What Is It to Draw the Limits of Moral Language?" *Philosophy* 84 (2009) 550–70.
Augustine. *Confessions and Enchiridion*. Translated and edited by Albert Outler. Philadelphia: Westminster, 1955.
Bonhoeffer Dietrich, *The Cost of Discipleship*, translated by R. H. Fuller. New York: Simon and Schuster, 1959.
Boone, Kathleen C. *The Bible Tells Them So*. New York: State University of New York, 1988.
Booth, Wayne. *The Rhetoric of Fiction*. Chicago: University of Chicago, 1961.
Brooks, David. "On Conquering Fear." *New York Times*, 3 April 2015.
Bunge, Gabriel. *Despondency: The Scriptural Teaching of Evagrius Ponticus on Acedia*, translated by Anthony P. Gythiel. New York: St. Vladimir's Seminary, 2012.
Campbell, Will D., and Richard C. Goode. *Crashing the Idols: The Vocation of Will D. Campbell (and any other Christian for that matter)*. Eugene, OR: Cascade, 2010.
Campbell, Will D. *Cecelia's Sin: A Novella*. Macon, GA: Mercer University, 1983.
———. *Forty Acres and a Goat*. Atlanta: Peachtree Pub Ltd. 1986.
———. "Whose Freedom?" 1965 manuscript. Will D. Campbell papers. McCain Library and Archives.
Carette, Jeremy R., ed. *Religion and Culture: Michel Foucault*. New York: Rutledge, 1999.
Carrol, Rory. "California Drought Threatens Luxe Beverly Hills Lawns and Swimming Pools." *The Guardian* (2015), http://www.theguardian.com/us-news/2015/apr/22/california-drought-beverly-hills-lawns-pools.
Castelli, Elizabeth A. and Hal Taussig. "Introduction: Drawing Large and Startling Figures: Reimagining Christian Origins by Painting like Picasso." In *Reimagining Christian Origins: A Colloquium Honoring Burton L. Mack.*, 3–22. Valley Forge, PA: Trinity International, 1996.
Chappell, Bill. "Warren Harding, We Hardly Knew Ye," (13 Aug 2015). http://www.npr.org/sections/thetwo-way/2015/08/13/432064123/warren-harding-we-hardly-knew-ye.
Clements, Olivier. *Roots of Christian Mysticism: Texts from the Patristic Era with Commentary*, 2nd Edition. London: New City, 2013.
Coates, Ta-Nehisi. *Between the World and Me*. New York: Spiegel & Grau, 2015.
Conroy, Pat. *My Reading Life*. New York: Random House, 2010.

BIBLIOGRAPHY

Corley, Kathleen E. *Women and the Historical Jesus: Feminist Myths of Christian Origins.* Santa Rosa, CA: Polebridge, 2002.

Crossan, Dominic. *Jesus: A Revolutionary Biography.* New York: HarperOne, 2009.

Davis, Ellen F. "Critical Traditioning." In *The Art of Reading Scripture*, edited by Ellen F. Davis and Richard B. Hayes, 163–80. Grand Rapids: William B. Eerdmans, 2003.

———. "Teaching the Bible Confessionally in the Church." In *The Art of Reading Scripture*, edited by Ellen F. Davis and Richard B. Hayes, 9–26. Grand Rapids: William B. Eerdmans, 2003.

Farb, Peter, and George Armelagos. *Consuming Passions: The Anthropology of Eating.* Boston: Houghton Mifflin, 1980.

Fiorenza, Elisabeth Schüssel. *In Memory of Her: A Feminist Theological Reconstruction of Christian Origins.* New York: Crossroads, 1994.

Fowl, Stephen E. *Engaging Scripture: A Model for Theological Interpretation.* Eugene, OR: Wipf & Stock; reprint edition, 2008.

Garcia-Navarro, Lourdes. "Dark-Skinned or Black? How Afro-Brazilians Are Forging a Collective Identity." *All Things Considered* (2015). http://www.npr.org/sections/codeswitch/2015/08/12/431244962/dark-skinned-or-black-how-afro-brazilians-are-forging-a-collective-identity.

Garland, David E. *The NIV Application Commentary: Mark.* Grand Rapids: Zondervan, 1996.

Grantham, Thomas. *Apology for the Baptized Believers.* London: Thomas Grantham, 1684

———. *Christianismus Primitivus, or The Ancient Christian Religion* Book II. London: n.p. 1678.

———. *The Prisoner Against the Prelate: Or, A Dialogue Between the Common Goal and the Cathedral of London.* London, 1662.

Gurganus, Allan. *White People.* New York: Vintage, 2000.

Harmon, Steven. *Baptist Identity and the Ecumenical Future: Story, Tradition, and the Recovery of Community.* Eugene, OR: Wipf & Stock, 2010.

Harris, Harriet A. *Fundamentalism and Evangelicals.* New York: Oxford University, 1998.

Hart, David Bentley. *The Doors of the Sea.* Grand Rapids, MI: William B. Eerdmans, 2005.

Hauerwas, Stanley. *In Good Company: The Church as Polis.* Notre Dame: The University of Notre Dame, 1995.

Hays, Richard B., and Ellen F. Davis. "Beyond Criticism: Learning to Read the Bible Again." *Christian Century* 121 (2004) 23–27.

Hebblethwaite, Brian, and Edward Henderson, eds. *Divine Action: Studies Inspired by the Philosophical Theology of Austin Farrer.* London: Bloomsbury T. & T. Clark, 2000.

Hyde, Lewis. *The Gift: Creativity and the Artist in the Modern World.* New York: Vintage; 25th Anniversary edition, 2007.

Katongole, Emmanuel. *The Sacrifice of Africa: A Political Theology for Africa.* Grand Rapids: Eerdmans, 2010.

Keck, Leander. *The Bible in the Pulpit.* Nashville: Abingdon, 1978.

Keller, *Jesus the King: Understanding the Life and Death of the Son of God.* New York: Riverhead Books, 2011.

Ketchin, Susan, edited *The Christ-Haunted Landscape: Faith and Doubt in Southern Literature.* Jackson, MS: University of Mississippi, 1994.

King, Martin Luther, Jr. Nobel Peace Prize acceptance speech. www.nobelprize.org/.../peace/laureates/1964/king-acceptance.html.

BIBLIOGRAPHY

Kraemer, Ross S. "Jewish Women and Christian Origins: Some Caveats." In *Women and Christian Origins*, edited by Ross Shepard Kraemer and Mary Rose D'Angelo, 35–49. Oxford: Oxford University, 1999.

Kugel, James L. *How to Read the Bible: A Guide to Scripture, Then and Now*. New York: Simon & Schuster, 2007.

Leonard, Bill J. "An Orthodox Creed, Or A Protestant Confession of Faith." In *Baptist Confessions of Faith*, edited by William L. Lumpkin and Bill J. Leonard, 298–348 . Valley Forge: Judson Press, 2011.

Mar, Gary. "Evangelization through Asian Eyes." Paper presented at *The Logic of Evangelism*. St Louis: Concordia Theological Seminary, 1994.

Marcus, Joel. *The Anchor Bible: Mark 1–8: A New Translation with Introduction and Commentary*. New Haven: Yale Press, 2000.

Marney, Carlyle. "A Come and Go Affair." *The Twentieth Century Pulpit*, edited James W. Cox. Nashville: Abingdon, 1978, 135–40.

Martin, Dale B. *Sex and the Single Savior: Gender and Sexuality in Biblical Interpretation*. Louisville: Westminster John Knox, 2006.

Maximus the Confessor, *Questions to Thalassius*. In Olivier Clément, *The Roots of Christian Mysticism: Texts from the Patristic Era with Commentary*, translated by Theodor Berkley, O.C.S.O. and Jeremy Hummerstone. London: New City, 1993.

McClendon, James W. *Doctrine: Systematic Theology, Vol. 2*. Nashville: Abingdon, 1994.

McElvaine, Robert S. *The Great Depression: America, 1929–1941*. New York: Three Rivers Press, 2009.

O'Connor, Flannery. *Mystery and Manners: Occasional Prose, Selected & Edited by Sally and Robert Fitzgerald*. New York: Farrar, Straus and Giroux, 1970.

———. *Wise Blood*. New York: Farrar, Straus and Giroux; Reissue edition. 2007.

Primack, Dan. "Donald Trump's Plan to Pay for Mexico Border Wall Has a Tech Problem." *Fortune* (17 Aug 2015). http://fortune.com/2015/08/17/donald-trumps-plan-to-pay-for-mexico-wall-has-a-tech-problem/.

Pseudo-Macarius. "Eighteenth Homily." In *Pseudo-Macarius: The Fifty Spiritual Homilies and the Great Letter*, edited by George A. Maloney, (141–46). New York: Paulist Press, 1992.

Sharp, Carolyn. *Irony and Meaning in the Hebrew Bible*. Loomington IN: Indiana University, 2008.

Smith, Christian. *The Bible Made Impossible: Why Biblicism Is Not a Truly Evangelical Reading of Scripture*. Grand Rapids: Brazos, 2012.

Smith, Lee. "Tongues of Fire." In *The Christ-Haunted Landscape*, edited by Susan Ketchin, 5–44. Jackson: University of Mississippi, 1994.

Stephens, Randall J., and Karl W. Giberson. *The Anointed: Evangelical Truth in a Secular Age*. Cambridge, MA: Harvard University, 2011.

Taylor, Barbara Brown. *When God Is Silent*. Cambridge, MA: Cowley Publication,1998.

Taylor, Charles. *A Secular Age*. Cambridge, MA: Harvard University, 2007.

Terrien, Samuel. "The Omphalos Myth and Hebrew Religion." In *Vetus Testamentum* 20, no. 3, (1970) 315–38.

Thuesen, Peter J. *In Discordance with the Scriptures: American Protestant Battles over Translating the Bible*. New York: Oxford University, 1999.

Wittgenstein, Ludwig. *Philosophical Investigations*. Edited by G. E. M. Anscombe and Rush Rhees, trans. G. E. M. Anscombe. New York: Macmillan, 1953.

BIBLIOGRAPHY

Worthen, Molly. *Apostles of Reason. The Crisis of Authority in American Evangelicalism.* New York: Oxford University, 2011.

Yoder, John Howard. "The Imperative of Christian Unity." In *The Royal Priesthood,* edited by Michael G. Cartwright. Huntington, 289 – 99. Scottdale, PA: Herald, 1994.

www.ingramcontent.com/pod-product-compliance
Lightning Source LLC
Chambersburg PA
CBHW071510150426
43191CB00009B/1465